'Mohammed Ayoob's short book is a brilliant analysis of Middle East politics. It makes for sobering, yet essential, reading.'

Patrick Seale, author of *The Struggle for Arab Independence: Riad el-Solh and the Makers of the Modern Middle East*

'Mohammed Ayoob is our most informed, judicious, perceptive, and insightful commentator on recent developments in the Middle East. He has now written an indispensable book that surveys the region as a whole while providing penetrating accounts of what is unfolding in each country, and how the play of forces from within and without is generating a crisis of potentially global proportions.'

Professor Richard Falk, Milbank Professor of International Law Emeritus, Princeton University, and UN Special Rapporteur on Occupied Palestine

WITHDRAWN

Will the Middle East Implode?

Mohammed Ayoob

WILL THE MIDDLE EAST IMPLODE?

polity

First published in 2014 by Polity Press

Polity Press
65 Bridge Street
Cambridge CB2 1UR, UK

Polity Press
350 Main Street
Malden, MA 02148, USA

ISBN-13: 978-0-7456-7924-2
ISBN-13: 978-0-7456-7925-9 (pb)

A catalogue record for this book is available from the British Library.

Typeset in 11 on 15 pt Sabon by
Servis Filmsetting Ltd, Stockport, Cheshire
Printed and bound in the United States by Edwards Brothers Malloy

The publisher has used its best endeavours to ensure that the URLs for external websites referred to in this book are correct and active at the time of going to press. However, the publisher has no responsibility for the websites and can make no guarantee that a site will remain live or that the content is or will remain appropriate.

For further information on Polity, visit our website:
www.politybooks.com

This book is dedicated to the scholars and staff of the Institute for Social Policy and Understanding (ISPU) in appreciation of their contribution to the objective study of Muslim Americans and America's relations with the Muslim world

Contents

Acknowledgements

The idea for this book came from Louise Knight, Senior Acquisitions Editor at Polity, who suggested to me that I should seriously consider the proposal and simultaneously offered me a contract to write it. Had it not been for her the book would never have been written. Justin Dyer did a fantastic job of editing the manuscript in record time. He went above and beyond the call of duty by constantly bringing to my attention unfolding events in the Middle East that could have a major bearing on the subjects that I have addressed in the book. I am grateful to Louise for the faith she reposed in me and to Justin for his superb handling of the manuscript. I am also grateful to the two anonymous reviewers of the initial draft who made very valuable comments that forced me to think harder about several themes covered in the book and to refine my arguments and

Acknowledgements

sharpen my conclusions. The scholars who have endorsed the book so generously also deserve my gratitude.

The Institute for Social Policy and Understanding (ISPU), to whose scholars and staff this book is dedicated, is an independent, nonpartisan think tank that operates out of Washington, DC, and Michigan. It is a unique research organization that has become a trusted source of information and analysis for the policy-making community, the media, and academia about Muslim Americans, Muslim societies around the world, and America's relations with key Muslim countries, especially in the Middle East and South Asia. I am grateful to ISPU for having enriched my intellectual life during the past decade that I have been associated with it as an adjunct scholar.

Mohammed Ayoob

1

After the Arab Spring

As the civil war in Syria continues to spill out of control, the security situation in Libya deteriorates further, the threat of secession in Yemen escalates, and the elected government in Egypt is overthrown by a military coup, it is hardly surprising that the legacy of the Arab Spring is hotly debated. But was the Arab Spring simply a mirage that will ultimately lead to disillusionment? Or were these uprisings really a harbinger of better times? So far the evidence would seem to give credence to the first interpretation, although enough of the spark of the original movements survives to make some analysts optimistic about the long-term future of the Arab world. What these discussions miss, however, is the real significance of the Arab uprisings: namely, the introduction of a huge amount of uncertainty in Middle Eastern politics that has upset the calculations of most regional and external actors and led to a highly fluid and potentially combustible state of affairs in this already volatile region.

Above all, the Arab uprisings have driven home the lesson that change in the Middle East not only is possible but also can occur with astonishing speed. The backlash that these upheavals have generated has also demonstrated the capacity of existing rulers, as in Syria and Bahrain, or recently overthrown regimes, as in Egypt, to mount counter-offensives that have effectively neutralized the early gains of the pro-change forces. This dialectic of revolution and counter-revolution witnessed since 2010, when combined with the existing challenges already facing the region, is capable of driving the Middle East toward not only greater instability but even possible implosion.

Despite the recent reversals faced by the proponents of regime transformation in the region, the Middle East, especially its Arab component, which had for decades appeared hide-bound and fossilized, is now galvanized as never before. Notwithstanding the fact that these upheavals occurred in discrete national contexts, they unfolded in the form of a chain reaction with uprisings in each Arab country acting as catalysts for similar upheavals in neighboring ones all the way from Tunisia to Bahrain. This pattern of events demonstrated the existence of an Arab "system" that transcends borders and is based on linguistic affinity and shared access to the Arab language media – in both its electronic and print forms. This phenomenon is very different from earlier attempts at unifying the Arab world under the banner of Arab nationalism that challenged existing borders of Arab states.

The current series of upheavals, while affirming the sense of affinity and empathy among Arab publics, has also affirmed the validity of state borders and existing sovereignties that divide the Arab world politically. There has been no attempt to unify the Arab world under the banner of the Arab Spring. In fact, there have been several discrete Springs: a Tunisian Spring, an Egyptian Spring, a Libyan Spring, and so on and so forth. Where the upheavals have threatened the territorial integrity of existing Arab states, for example Syria, it is because of the actions of certain elements of the population that are likely to lose out in the process of political transition and creation of new national orders.

Finer points apart, it is clear that things in the Middle East can no longer be considered immutable, whether it is the nature of regimes, intra-societal balances, or relationships among states. Moreover, since the three arenas of regimes, societies, and inter-state relations are not immune to mutual influences, change or the prospect of change in one arena is likely to have major impact on the others as well.

This is why it is important to analyze the Arab Spring in the context of the major problems facing the Middle East today, especially since the uncertainties introduced by the Arab upheavals can act as significant transforming agents in these problem areas, several of which are simultaneously coming to a boil. Given these interconnections and overlaps, there appears to be a serious danger of a chain reaction developing and leading to an implosion, or a number of mini-implosions, that could engulf much of the region. Such a domino effect could lead to state failure and sectarian warfare with region-wide implications in strategically important countries such as Syria and Iraq, the latter already de-stabilized by the American occupation and its violent aftermath. It could also lead to civil strife engendered by irreconcilable rifts on the nature of emerging political orders, as is already happening in the largest Arab state, Egypt. Inter-state conflict might also follow: for example, between Israel and Iran on Israel's insistence on maintaining its regional nuclear monopoly and the Iranian pursuit of nuclear enrichment, which could have military implications.

All these scenarios have the capacity to draw external powers into regional conflicts and turn the latter into major global security issues. Some of this is happening already, as in the case of the Iranian nuclear program and the Syrian civil war. The fact that the Middle East, especially its Persian Gulf sub-region, is home to approximately 60 percent of the planet's oil reserves and about 40 percent of its natural gas reserves makes the situation even more combustible thanks to a perennially energy-starved world that intimately ties the health of industrial and industrializing economies to issues of conflict and order in this volatile region.

Five key sources of potential combustion can be seen in the region today: (1) the growing role of political Islam and the anti-Islamist backlash; (2) the enduring Israel–Palestine conflict and its increasingly zero-sum nature; (3) Iran's quest for nuclear capability, the potential challenge this poses to Israel's nuclear monopoly in the Middle East, and the Israeli–American threat of military action against Iran's nuclear facilities; (4) heightened rivalry among regional powers, especially Iran, Saudi Arabia, and Turkey, manifested starkly in their stance on the Syrian civil war; and (5) great power interests and involvement, clearly demonstrated by the American invasion and occupation of Iraq, which have the potential to turn regional conflagrations into global confrontations. As we will see, the conflict-potential of several of these issues has been amplified by the impact of the Arab uprisings and the uncertainties introduced by them.

The world had come to live with some of these problems (or so one thought until recently). The impasse between Israel and the Palestinians and the perennial issue of access to the energy resources of the Persian Gulf have been familiar causes of conflict for the past few decades. Others, such as the resurgence of political Islam and the stand-off between Israel and Iran on the former's insistence that Tehran give up its nuclear enrichment program, are relatively new but ones which the international community has been struggling to address for the past several years. Yet others, especially those related to prospects of state debilitation if not state failure directly generated by the Arab Spring, although foreshadowed by the near-total collapse of the Iraqi state following the American invasion of 2003, are very new and the international community is still struggling to find ways of coping with them. The dramatic resurfacing of regional rivalries as a consequence of the Arab upheavals, most clearly apparent in the context of the Syrian civil war, has also caught the international community off-guard and heightened prospects of conflict and instability in this unstable part of the world.

But what is new even about the older issues, such as Israel–Palestine and the Iranian nuclear program, is that they are now coming to a head for a number of reasons, some regional, some global. Israel, ever more nervous about its future in a Middle East that is democratizing (or so it appeared until the military coup in Egypt in July 2013), has increasingly focused its paranoia on Iran's nuclear enrichment program. It is also, one might contend, a convenient ploy to divert international attention from the plight of the Palestinians under occupation and the continuing Jewish colonization of Palestinian lands. Israeli leaders have become increasingly shrill in their insistence that Iran is about to cross an Israel-imposed "red line" by acquiring the technological capability to manufacture nuclear weapons and needs to be stopped, by war if necessary.

The American position on the issue, although more nuanced than its Israeli counterpart, basically supports the Israeli contention and has put Washington at odds with Tehran and with Muslim opinion (although not necessarily with Muslim regimes such as Saudi Arabia) not only in the

Middle East but also around the world. An Israeli or an Israeli–American attack on Iran's nuclear facilities is likely to have far-reaching consequences for the region and for the global economy, hardening Muslim animosity against the United States and dramatically raising energy prices, thus destabilizing the political as well as the economic equilibrium of an increasingly fragile international system.[1]

The Arab Spring has both charged and changed the atmosphere in the Middle East and breathed new life into the Palestinian resistance to Israeli occupation and colonization, thus reviving the need for a quick and just solution to the conflict before it embroils this part of the world in yet another region-wide war. The spirit of the Arab Spring is bound to reach occupied Palestine (probably in the form of the third *intifada*), and indeed, some argue, the Arab population of Israel itself, sooner rather than later. The Israeli policy of colonizing the West Bank, while ostensibly seeking a two-state solution, is increasingly turning the Israel–Palestine conflict into an irresolvable contradiction with momentous consequences for the Israeli polity itself. The extremely intransigent stand adopted by important members of the current Israeli government, advocating not only continuing Jewish settlement but also annexation of 60 percent of the West Bank and declaring that Palestinian statehood is at a "dead-end," make a third *intifada* almost inevitable.[2]

The Arab Spring has also re-ignited the debate about the role of political Islam in a democratizing Middle East, with protagonists arguing its positive and negative aspects. This is the case because Islamist parties, as in Tunisia and Egypt, are the best-organized political machines and, therefore, were able to come to power either by themselves or in coalition with others in post-authoritarian contexts. The fact that mainstream Islamist movements and parties, such as Ennahda in Tunisia, the Muslim Brotherhood in Egypt, and the PJD in Morocco, enthusiastically embraced the democratic process is seen as a very positive development by more optimistic commentators. More critical observers, however, argue that the impressive electoral performance of the Islamist parties is likely to have regressive implications for Arab societies and highly negative consequences for the Arab world's relations with the West.[3] No matter where one stands in this debate, it is clear that the transformation of Islamist movements into governing parties is likely to have major implications for the region. The removal of these parties from office by force, as happened in Egypt in July 2013, is likely to have even graver consequences both for the future of democracy and for the future of Islamist moderation in the Middle East.

The Arab Spring has had, and will continue to have, different outcomes in different countries of the region. While it appeared until recently that the Tunisian transition had gone somewhat smoothly, it has run into major obstacles thanks in great part to the intransigent nature of the secular opposition and the extremist proclivities of salafist elements in the Tunisian polity. The Egyptian transition not only created deep rifts within the country but also led to a counter-revolution in the form of a military coup that overthrew the country's first elected President and was followed by a massacre of at least one thousand of his supporters. The coup and its aftermath have signaled that the most populous Arab state is likely to undergo instability and civil strife of a pretty high order for an extended period of time.

The Arab Spring has demonstrated that it is easier to overthrow old orders than to put new ones in their place. Libya almost descended into anarchy, from which it has been pulled back at least temporarily through the the sagacity of its leadership. However, the spillover of regime change in Libya on neighboring countries, such as Algeria and Mali, could turn out to be highly de-stabilizing. Syria has not been as fortunate as Libya. There is a better than even chance that if the Assad regime falls, Syria will be divided up into ethnic- and sectarian-based mini-states in constant conflict with each other. It is already becoming clear that the strife in Syria has had tremendous negative impact, especially in the arena of inter-sectarian relations, upon the neighboring states of Lebanon and Iraq, which are also fractured societies, and that this is turning the Fertile Crescent into a perpetual conflict zone.

So, as the following chapters will show, all or most of these sources of conflict in the Middle East are inter-related and the Arab uprisings have only served to bind them more tightly, with the various forms of conflict feeding upon each other and thereby pushing the entire region closer to implosion. Whether political sagacity and diplomatic creativity can bring the Middle East back from the brink remains to be seen.

2

The Islamist Challenge

Islamism and Islamists are broad umbrella terms that hide as much as they reveal. At the most general level, Islamism refers to a vague political ideology that asserts that Islam, in some shape or form, should guide the constitutional framework and policies of states with predominantly Muslim populations. Islamist parties and movements crystallized during the twentieth century largely as a result of Muslim societies' interaction from a position of weakness with the West. Their diagnosis of the ills of Muslim societies that led to the latter's domination by European powers was that these societies, and especially their elites, had moved away from the basic norms of Islamic behavior and that their weakness was the result of this fundamental shortcoming. Their prescription was that if Islamic codes of behavior could be reintroduced into the political lives of their countries, Muslim societies would regain their former strength and position of glory. Islamist movements were, therefore, as much products of modernity as they were reactions to it.

However, given the politically and socially fractured nature of the Muslim world, Islamist movements, where they arose, became prisoners of their own social and political contexts. Different leadership styles and intellectual convictions also added to the diversity of Islamist movements. Consequently, these movements and their leaderships ended up interpreting the general Islamist dictum relating to the relevance of Islam to political life in manifold ways and covering a broad spectrum of convictions. Such diversity helped make Islamist movements and parties relevant in their national contexts but at the same time exploded the myth of the Islamist monolith.[1]

This broad spectrum of Islamist parties and movements includes mainstream political parties, such as the Ennahda (Renaissance) of Tunisia and the Muslim Brotherhood of Egypt and the latter's offshoots in other Arab countries. These parties, like their post-Islamist cousin the Justice and Development Party (AKP) of Turkey, are primarily Islamically inspired political machines whose main objective is to build broad coalitions to capture political power in order to infuse the functioning of the state with Islamic societal values. Although some of them, such as the Muslim Brotherhood, are ostensibly committed to the introduction of sharia law, they are willing to make compromises that relegate this to the status of a long-term goal that may or may not attain fruition. Others, such as the AKP, have jettisoned this goal totally and publicly and committed themselves to upholding the values of the secular state while preserving Islamic societal norms. Ennahda of Tunisia seems to be moving in a similar direction.

Islamist movements also include the salafis, the Muslim equivalents of the Puritans or Fundamentalists of Christendom, who follow strict and literalist codes of Islamic conduct and pattern their behavior on the example set by the first generation of pious Muslims – the salaf-al-salih or righteous ancestors. Most of these groups are either apolitical or adopt peaceful methods of persuasion to change society and influence politics. Some of them, such as the al-Nour Party in Egypt, in a dramatic departure from earlier patterns of behavior, have lately entered the realm of competitive politics in the wake of the Arab upheavals.

At the fringes – and they form a minuscule part of

the Islamist universe – Islamist movements include militant, extremist formations, many of whom are grouped under the term salafi as well but diverge from the salafis in very important ways. They are Leninist organizations that are products of hybridization between social conservatism and political radicalism, whose primary objectives are political rather than religious or social. These militant groups are not averse to engaging in violent acts to achieve their political ends. They are popularly known as "jihadis," a perversion of the term "mujahidin" (those who fight in the way of God), but one that has no Islamic significance whatsoever. However, it has become popular in journalistic and even academic discourse in the West. This category includes both national jihadis who aim at violently overthrowing local regimes, the "near enemy," and transnational jihadis, above all al-Qaeda and its affiliates, who have global agendas and whose primary target is the "far enemy," the United States and its Western allies.[2]

Western skepticism and suspicion

It is worth noting, however, that the history of even mainstream, non-radical Islamist parties' relationship with the West, and especially with the United States, has been at best rocky and at worst hostile. This is why the emergence of mainstream Islamist parties in the wake of the Arab Spring as major political players and in some cases as leading members of governing coalitions, as in Egypt and Tunisia, set off alarm bells in many quarters, especially in the United States. These include conservative and staunchly pro-Israel segments of American opinion traditionally wary of Islamist parties and movements because they believe that anti-American and anti-Israeli sentiments are embedded in the Islamists' genes.

Even liberal Western analysts of the Middle Eastern scene have expressed strong reservations about the Islamist parties because of what they see as the tendency among mainstream Islamists, epitomized by some of the policies of the Egyptian Muslim Brotherhood, to make compromises with elements of the old order, particularly the military top brass, to ensure the Islamists' smooth accession to office at the cost of the revolutions' objectives. While this strategy failed in Egypt, where the military overthrew the elected government in July 2013, it did leave the impression that the Muslim Brotherhood was willing to sacrifice long-term democratic goals for immediate political gain.

Furthermore, segments of Arab populations that consider themselves secular and/or liberal as well as remnants of the old regimes displaced by the uprisings express strong skepticism about the objectives, intentions, and tactics of the Islamist parties as the latter move toward the centers of political power. It was this combination of holdovers from the Mubarak regime and liberal-secular elements in the Egyptian polity that led to the military coup against President Morsi's government, with the liberals providing political cover for the military brass's self-serving motives.

Criticism and disquiet over mainstream Islamist parties stem from two key concerns: firstly, the Islamist parties' apparently skin-deep commitment to democratic principles, famously expressed by the phrase "one person, one vote, one time"; secondly, the mainstream Islamists' penchant for anti-Western and anti-Israeli rhetoric that their Western critics fear will eventually be translated into policy, such as removal of American military bases from countries hosting them, suspension or even revocation of peace treaties with Israel, and political and military support to groups such as the Palestinian Hamas and the Lebanese Hizbullah that have been declared terrorist organizations by the United States.

The first concern owes much to the statements

and writings of some of the leading figures who dominated the Islamist political and intellectual universe during the first half of the twentieth century. Sayyid Qutb, the Egyptian Brotherhood's chief ideologue in the 1950s and 1960s, epitomized this group. These ideologues advocated the sovereignty of God (*hakimiyya*), denied the full sovereignty of the people, circumscribed the legislative powers of people's assemblies, and subjected human-made constitutional provisions to the test of compatibility with the commands of God.[3]

But Islamist movements have evolved a great deal from the time when Qutb dominated the Islamist intellectual universe. He is no longer considered the philosopher par excellence of the Muslim Brotherhood, and his most controversial ideas, especially those that seemed to advocate violent overthrow of existing regimes in the Arab world, were indirectly refuted by the Supreme Guide of the Brotherhood as early as 1969, soon after Qutb's execution in 1966, and directly in 1982. In the latter year the Supreme Guide of the Muslim Brotherhood declared unequivocally that "Sayyid Qutb represented himself and not the Muslim Brethren."[4] Moreover, Qutb's writings have been variously interpreted by succeeding generations of Islamists. Both moderates and extremists (inside and outside the Brotherhood) have used his writings to justify their own agendas. This is the case because Qutb's ideas were still evolving when he was executed by President Nasser in 1966, and therefore lend themselves to multiple and differing interpretations.

The evolution of the mainstream Islamists' approach toward moderation and political participation clearly witnessed in the case of the Egyptian Muslim Brotherhood is visible across the spectrum of Islamist parties. This has been particularly the case where political systems such as Jordan and Morocco, even though insufficiently democratic, have liberalized enough to provide greater opportunities for political participation. Transformations in their approach to politics that have taken place in the Muslim Brotherhood's Jordanian branch, the Islamic Action Front (IAF), and in the Justice and Development Party (PJD) in Morocco demonstrate the validity of this thesis. The most dramatic example is that of the Justice and Development Party (AKP), the current ruling party in Turkey, heir to the Islamist political tradition in that country. It broke away from the old mold of Islamist politics in 2001 and has transformed itself into a party that is post-Islamist ("conservative democratic," to use the phrase favored by its leadership) and has become the prime vehicle for the consolidation of Turkish democracy. In the process it has reversed the balance in civilian–military relations hugely in favor of the former.

In fact, even before the Arab uprisings, more optimistic analysts and commentators took their cue from the demonstrated ideological flexibility and pragmatic political behavior of mainstream Islamist movements and their increasing commitment to peaceful political action despite repression by authoritarian and semi-authoritarian regimes. Consequently, they were and continue to be much more sanguine about the Islamists' commitment to democratic constitutionalism. The gradual socialization of the Islamist parties into democratic and semi-democratic systems, they contend, helps these parties to internalize democratic values because acquiring and holding power necessitates compromises, induces pragmatism, and leads to moderation, defined as the willingness to accept democratic norms of political participation, including non-violent opposition, respect for the results of free and fair elections, and willingness to give up power if voted out of office. The fact that in several cases the Islamically rooted parties have become the main champions of democratic governance seems to support this view.

Another Western criticism of the intermingling of religion and politics in the Middle East is based on commentators' unease that, unlike present-day Western Europe and North America, there is no clear demarcation between the religious and political spheres in the Muslim world, which strengthens Islamist political forces that employ religious idioms and use religious institutions to further their political agendas. While this criticism is valid up to a certain point, it ignores four major facts. First, the historical trajectory of church–state relations in the Middle East has been very different from that in Europe. There has never been a central religious authority in Islam *à la* the Pope whom temporal rulers had to confront in order to vindicate their sovereign authority. In the process, in some European countries the church came to be perceived as the foremost enemy of the new sovereign state whose opposition had to be overcome by forced secularization and control of the church by the temporal rulers.

Second, there have been no major wars of religion within Islam on the scale seen in Europe between Catholics and Protestants that required the secularization of polities and in several cases the imposition of state control over religion. Therefore, the need to separate religion from politics has never been perceived as a major priority in Muslim societies, which have historically been far more tolerant than Europe was until the twentieth century of religious and sectarian differences.

Third, Islam as interpreted by scholars toiling away in their seminaries outside the control of the state in the pre-modern period imposed limits on the arbitrary use of state power, and therefore protected individual and group rights in the classical period of Islamic history. All the five major schools of Islamic jurisprudence emerged as a result of scholarship undertaken by the *ulama* within civil society. Religion was, therefore, seen as an ally of the people, especially of the downtrodden, and not merely as an instrument to legitimize state authority. This tradition continues to influence the oppositional politics of Islamist movements around the world today.

Fourth, the current strength of the Islamist parties in the Middle East is a direct result of the fact that authoritarian regimes in power for decades decimated all secular opposition and thereby created a political void into which the Islamists were able to move and position themselves as the primary opponents of tyrannical orders. Moreover, since these authoritarian regimes often projected a secular-nationalist image, secularism was seen as an adjunct of authoritarianism while Islam was perceived as a vehicle for democratization and the preservation of civil rights. Above all, given the weakness of secular parties long suppressed or co-opted by authoritarian regimes, Islamist parties were the only ones that possessed organizational strength and popular credibility in countries such as Tunisia and Egypt. It should have come as no surprise, therefore, that they performed better than their secular counterparts in the first round of elections following the overthrow of despotic regimes in several Arab countries.

In fact, it is the combination of these factors that explains the current electoral strength of Islamist parties in the Middle East. However, this situation is unlikely to last very long as democratization, if allowed to proceed without hindrance, increasingly levels the playing field between Islamists and their secular opponents. It may even redound to the latter's benefit if they demonstrate adequate patience and let the political credibility of Islamist governments be undermined by their performance or non-performance. However, if secular movements attempt to de-stabilize duly elected Islamist governments by extra-constitutional means and support the remnants of the old regimes in overthrowing Islamist governments, as they did in Egypt in July

2013, they are likely to end up increasing popular sympathy for Islamist parties that had attained office as a result of the electoral mandate. The overthrow of the Muslim Brotherhood government in Egypt by the military could actually prove to be to the Brotherhood's long-term advantage if participatory politics is revived in the country. Conversely, it may lead to disillusionment on the part of a segment of mainstream Islamists with the democracy route and encourage them to adopt violent means, thus vindicating the extremists' argument that Islamist parties will never be allowed to attain and retain power through non-violent and democratic means – a theme we will return to in the concluding chapter of the book.

The decline of Islamist militancy

It is instructive to note, however, that in several cases democracy movements in the Middle East with heavy participation by mainstream Islamist parties have clearly demonstrated that the extremist and violent manifestations of Islamism, including its transnational version al-Qaeda, remain marginal to the unfolding political processes in the Muslim world.[5] This does not mean that they have totally disappeared from the scene, as the resurgence of al-Qaeda affiliates in the wake of revolution and civil war in Libya and Syria clearly show. It does mean, however, that violent and militant Islamism is firmly on the wane and plays second fiddle to mainstream Islamist *political* parties. Militant Islamism becomes prominent only in contexts of severe state failure, as was the case in Afghanistan and Iraq and as now threatens Libya, Syria, and Yemen. Without the collapse or debilitation of state authority, militant groups, including transnational ones, do not have the territorial and political space to put down roots and flourish.

The difference between the latest burst of al-Qaeda-linked activities and the initial thrust of al-Qaeda's activities from the mid-1990s to 2001 is quite clear. In the earlier phase al-Qaeda was obsessed with fighting the United States and its Western allies. This changed dramatically after 2001 with the decimation of al-Qaeda's central command in Afghanistan and the liquidation and/or dispersal of much of its top leadership. Al-Qaeda franchises in Iraq, Yemen, Saudi Arabia, Pakistan, and elsewhere, while retaining some of the original transnational rhetoric, became engaged in struggles that were principally national or sub-national in character. This transformation has been taken to its logical conclusion in the wake of the Arab uprisings, with al-Qaeda affiliates in Libya, Algeria, Mali, Yemen, and elsewhere clearly engaged in local battles often for territorial control within existing states. This is a far cry from the pristine transnational objectives espoused by al-Qaeda in its formative phase under Bin Laden.

Given the prevalence of anti-Western, especially anti-American, public sentiment in the Middle East, it is understandable that popularly elected governments, whether Islamist or not, are likely to be more critical of Western/American policies than were their authoritarian predecessors. They argue, however, that this has to do more with American policy in the Middle East, especially Washington's reputation for propping up authoritarian regimes and its uncritical support for Israel's policies of occupation and colonization of Palestinian territories, than with primordial loathing for American political values. Poll after poll in the Middle East has demonstrated close overlap between American political values and those of the publics polled in the Middle East. The outbreak of democracy movements simultaneously in several Arab countries, the consolidation of democracy in Turkey, and the surprising outcome of the 2013 Presidential elections in Iran all testify to the commitment of Middle Eastern people to democratic values and to their efforts to pry out political space even in difficult circumstances, such as in Iran, to express popular will.

Counter-revolutionary political Islam

So, as we have seen, political manifestations of Islam are very diverse and the various expressions of Islamism are products of their social and political milieus as well as of the agendas of those groups and political actors who use Islam as an instrument to achieve their worldly ends. But this discussion of Islamists and their likely impact on the political landscape of the Middle East is not complete unless one includes within it the counter-revolutionary version of political Islam espoused by the Saudi establishment and aimed at protecting the regime's interests and those of its allies within the region.

It is instructive to note that in the era of democratic uprisings in the Arab world, Saudi Arabia has been using its Islamist credentials in a very cynical manner: for example, supporting the Syrian opposition to Assad's authoritarian regime while leading the counter-revolutionary charge against democratic change elsewhere in the Arab world. This is particularly true in the Persian Gulf sub-region of the Middle East that the Saudi regime aspires to dominate through its vast oil wealth, its dominant physical presence on the Arab littoral of the Persian Gulf, its alliance with the Wahhabi religious establishment, and its close political and security linkage with the United States.

When reverberations of the Arab Spring reached Saudi Arabia in 2011, the Saudi religious establishment, following the dictates of the regime, issued a *fatwa* (religious opinion) that declared it un-Islamic to oppose Saudi rule. Simultaneously, the Saudi security establishment came down heavily against participants in the sporadic protests that took place in the predominantly Shia eastern part of the kingdom. It also moved to silence Saudi human rights activists by awarding long jail terms to some of the more well known among them who had dared to defy the regime by calling for a constitutional monarchy and using social media to agitate for the protection of civil liberties. Concurrently, King Abdullah announced subventions for Saudi citizens amounting to $130 billion to buy support for and stave off opposition to his rule.

Saudi Arabia's role as the leader of the counter-revolutionary brigade in the Middle East became very clear when Riyadh used the fig-leaf of the Gulf Cooperation Council (GCC) to intervene militarily in March 2011 to help the al-Khalifa ruling house in next-door Bahrain violently crush the democratic uprising in the tiny island. The Saudis and their Gulf allies deliberately propagated the myth that the uprising in Bahrain was a result of a Shiite-Iranian plot. By giving the uprising a sectarian color and by invoking the myth of Iranian conspiracy, the Sunni ruling houses of the Gulf attempted to secure the support of the predominantly Sunni populations of the Middle East.

That the Saudis intervened to help the Bahraini regime to suppress a democratic movement that was initially non-sectarian in character without any significant protest from the United States demonstrated Washington's collusion in this endeavor to protect a regime in Bahrain that hosts the headquarters of the US Fifth Fleet. It also demonstrated Washington's proclivity to kowtow to the political preferences of Saudi Arabia, its major ally in the energy-rich Gulf, on matters relating to the security of the region. This stance flew in the face of President Obama's public position supporting the pro-democracy movements in the Middle East, thus leaving the United States wide open to the charge of hypocrisy.

However, America was not the only one using double standards. Saudi Arabia, while crushing the democratic movement in Bahrain, was eager to see the toppling of Qaddafi, whom the Saudi regime hated because of his reported involvement in an earlier plot to assassinate the Saudi king. The Saudis and their despotic Gulf allies also threw their considerable financial and political weight behind the forces opposing the Assad regime in Syria. It was clear that the Saudi regime was not moved to action in Syria by its love for democracy. What galvanized Saudi support for the opposition was the fact that the Syrian regime is an ally of Riyadh's archrival in the Persian Gulf, Tehran. We will return to this subject later in the book when we discuss the regional balance of power in the Middle East and how this has been impacted by the Arab uprisings.

The West is worried about the populist form of Islamism as represented by the Muslim Brotherhood because it is afraid that its electoral success will have negative effects on the Western powers' interests in the Middle East. Simultaneously, Western, especially American, policy-makers consider the counter-revolutionary form of Islamism espoused by Saudi Arabia to be an ally of Western interests thanks in part to the Saudi control of vast oil resources, its position as the swing producer of crude, its close strategic ties to the United States and its allies, its policy of keeping forces of revolutionary change in check on the Arab littoral of the Persian Gulf, and its potential to balance Iran in the Persian Gulf region as well as in the broader Middle East.[6]

America's benign perception of Saudi Wahhabi Islamism, although somewhat damaged in the immediate aftermath of 9/11, has a long history dating back to the beginnings of oil exploration in the kingdom in the 1930s and the setting up of ARAMCO. This perception was strengthened in the 1950s and 1960s when the Saudis became the principal defenders of the West's interests in the Middle East in the face of the rising tide of Arab nationalism led by Nasser of Egypt that challenged Western, especially American, hegemony in the region. Saudi fundamentalism also acted as the primary ally of the United States during the campaign in the 1980s to oust the Soviet Union from Afghanistan.

Transnational jihadism

However, as the terrorist attacks of 9/11 and subsequent events demonstrated, Saudi Wahhabi Islamism had and continues to have a major downside in terms of Western interests in the Middle East. Of the 19 hijackers on that fateful day, 15 were from Saudi Arabia and it was clear that they and al-Qaeda in general were motivated by an anti-American ideology that was a hybrid of Wahhabi religious fundamentalism and Qutbist political radicalism. This hybrid ideology had found fertile ground in Saudi Arabia as early as the 1970s when the followers of Sayyid Qutb found refuge there having escaped the Nasserite regime's repression in Egypt. Riyadh welcomed them as part of its then ongoing cold war with Cairo and provided them influential positions in the Saudi educational system. These disciples of Qutb were able to influence a generation of students that came of age in Saudi Arabia's ultra-conservative social milieu but was disenchanted with the Kingdom's pro-Western foreign policy and the Saudi princes' lavish and un-Islamic life-style, both of which they felt compromised the fundamental tenets of Wahhabi Islam.

This hybridization produced a radical form of Wahhabism that became the mortal enemy of the establishment Wahhabism that was allied with the Saudi regime and was a major pillar of the political and social status quo in the Kingdom. This oppositional ideology surfaced dramatically in 1979 with the seizure of the Grand Mosque in Mecca – Islam's holiest site – by a group of radical Wahhabis who denounced the Saudi regime and the allied religious establishment for having compromised the pristine ideals of Wahhabi Islam. While the Saudis with French help were able to kill or capture (and later execute) most of the group implicated in the seizure of the Grand Mosque, this outcome merely pushed the radical Wahhabi tendency underground, only to resurface in the 1990s in the wake of the deployment of American forces on Saudi soil following the Iraqi invasion of Kuwait in 1990.[7]

In the meantime this hybrid ideology had attracted international adherents thanks to the "jihad" launched against the Soviet military intervention in Afghanistan undertaken with Saudi money and American arms and with Pakistan acting as the conduit for both. Al-Qaeda emerged as the unintended product of this jihadi enterprise as it found fertile ground to grow and prosper in an Afghanistan that descended into anarchy following the Soviet withdrawal in 1989 and the fall of the Marxist regime in 1992. The organization, now the global manifestation of hybrid radical Wahhabism, had both the United States and the Saudi regime in its cross-hairs. The latter, which had used the Wahhabi religious ideology to legitimize its rule, was finally hoisted with its own petard.

Although, as we've already mentioned, the efficacy and reach of al-Qaeda's central command and the attraction of its transnational ideological thrust were drastically reduced following the American and allied invasion of Afghanistan in 2001, the al-Qaeda phenomenon has not disappeared entirely. Post-2001 it has instead metamorphosed into a loose network of networks that is divided into regional and national franchises with little or no control by the central command, which itself has become an illusive if not an illusory body. In most cases, militant Islamist organizations have appropriated the title "al-Qaeda" with suitable regional suffixes – "of Iraq," "of the Islamic Maghreb," "of the Arabian Peninsula" – before this imprimatur has been awarded to them by the central leadership. But this has meant, again as has been stated above, that their objectives have become primarily regional and national even though they pay lip service to al-Qaeda's founding ideology of global jihad. In the final analysis, local logic has trumped global ideology.

Although al-Qaeda affiliates continue to remain marginal to the upheavals going on in the Middle East, for reasons spelled out earlier, they do tend to become somewhat prominent in those countries that suffer from state enfeeblement and are threatened with state failure. Yemen, Syria, and Libya (with its extension in Mali) are the major examples of this phenomenon but not the only ones.

The Islamist Challenge

The killing of American Ambassador Christopher Stevens in Benghazi, Libya, in September 2012 was a clear indication of the al-Qaeda-linked militants' capacity to inflict damage on foreign missions considered close to the new Libyan authorities. It is also likely that if upheavals threaten state capacity in other Arab countries without necessarily leading to swift democratic transformations, then al-Qaeda-like organizations will increasingly try to fill the political void in competition with ethnic and sectarian groups engaged in the same enterprise. This seems to be already happening in Syria, with the al-Qaeda-inspired Nusra Front acting as one of the major elements among the armed opposition to the Assad regime. Given the current repression of the Muslim Brotherhood, including repeated massacres of its supporters, by the military regime in Egypt, it may not be too far-fetched to imagine the emergence of an "al-Qaeda on the Nile" in that country.

These al-Qaeda-type groups also have the latent capacity of linking up with similar ones across porous borders both in North Africa and in the Fertile Crescent and creating mayhem, as the interlinked cases of violence in Libya, Algeria, and Mali, on the one hand, and Iraq and Syria, on the other, clearly demonstrate. Nonetheless, despite their recent resurgence in countries where state structures have been gravely damaged, militant Islamists, whether linked to al-Qaeda or not, continue to be marginal actors as far as the Arab upheavals are concerned. While their capacity for dramatic acts of violence should not be underrated, they remain bit players in the context of the Arab uprisings as compared to mainstream Islamist parties, such as the Muslim Brotherhood or even the salafist al-Nour Party in Egypt and Ennahda in Tunisia, which are in a position to shape the destinies of their nations by their acts of omission and commission.

Moreover, salafi movements such as the al-Nour Party in Egypt and the Ansar a-Sharia in Tunisia, from among whom the militants are likely to find recruits, either have bought into the democracy framework, as is the case with the former, or are primarily engaged in *dawa* (missionary work aimed at making Muslims better Muslims) and social and charitable activities, as is the case with the latter. This has considerably decreased the pull of militant jihadism in those Arab countries that have experienced democratic transformations. However, the recent coup in Egypt that overthrew the Morsi government may be once again increasing the attraction of jihadi elements among disillusioned mainstream

Islamists. We will have to wait and see if this happens.

There is a major in-built contradiction between the interests of the mainstream Islamists and the militant groups that fall under the al-Qaeda umbrella. The mainstream Islamist parties want to be seen as legitimate political players capable of governing their polities, whereas the militant groups are more interested in creating anarchy and mayhem than in providing alternative visions of governance. Hence mainstream Islamist parties are often the targets of militants' attacks because, when in government, as in Tunisia and previously in Egypt, they are the ones responsible for suppressing the violent activities of these al-Qaeda-linked groups. When not in government, as in the case of the Syrian Muslim Brotherhood, they are the main competitors for the political space that the militant Islamists aspire to capture. Confusing these two sets of very distinct actors does not do any service to our understanding of the Islamist phenomenon in the Middle East and beyond.

Shia Islamism

Similarly, confusing mainstream Sunni Islamist parties and their Shia counterparts in the Arab world

– Dawa, the Sadrists, and the Islamic Supreme Council in Iraq (ISCI), Hizbullah in Lebanon, and al-Wefaq in Bahrain – and painting them with the same broad brush does not serve the cause of analytical clarity. The Shia parties and movements must be understood on their own terms and in their own contexts, especially since their relations with the Sunni Islamist parties are often tense if not hostile. Like the Sunni Islamists, the Shia mainstream Islamists have also played significant roles in the Arab uprisings and in the politics surrounding these upheavals.

The moderate Shia party al-Wefaq in Bahrain initially had been the lead player in the democratic mobilization against the island's authoritarian al-Khalifa regime and suffered greatly for it. Once that uprising was given a sectarian color by the machinations of the regime, Shia clerics also came to play a significant role in the protest movement, thus turning the sectarian propaganda emanating from the Saudi and Bahraini regimes into a self-fulfilling prophecy. However, it seems that during the course of 2012 the leadership of the anti-regime movement was taken over by young and increasingly radicalized Shiites who considered al-Wefaq to be too ready to compromise with the regime and the clerics as too out of touch with the demands of the

Shia youth. This radicalization was prompted by the increasingly hard line adopted by the al-Khalifa regime, which closed the doors to a negotiated settlement of the crisis in Bahrain.[8]

Even before the current round of upheavals in the Arab world, the Shia parties in Iraq played significant roles in the transition to democracy following the American invasion. This so impressed the only American neo-conservative analyst knowledgeable in the affairs of the Middle East that as early as 2004 he concluded that the Shiite clerics and the Sunni fundamentalists were the most likely vehicles for the spread of democracy in the Arab world.[9] The Shia religious parties continue to be the dominant partners in the current Iraqi coalition government, even though they often work at cross-purposes with each other. In fact, in March 2008 a major intra-Shia battle raged between the ISCI- and Dawa-dominated government of Nouri al-Maliki, supported by the United States, and the more radical Sadrists, representing the urban underclass, for the control of Basra, Iraq's main port, and its oil-rich hinterland. It ended with an Iranian-brokered cease-fire.[10]

Political conflict, with mounting security implications, has escalated since al-Maliki's re-election as Prime Minister in 2010, despite the fact that his party came second to al-Iraqiyya, the cross-sectarian coalition led by former Prime Minister Ayad Allawi. Al-Maliki has increasingly concentrated power in his hands by using various extra-constitutional mechanisms, alienating not merely the Sunni Arabs and the Kurds but several Shia factions as well. His policies have resulted in growing threats of separatism by the Kurdish leadership and rising inter-sectarian violence, especially suicide attacks by Sunni extremists on soft Shia targets, such as pilgrims visiting Shia shrines. Shia Islamism in Iraq has at least in part become an instrument for personal power-grab by al-Maliki, thus discrediting Shia Islamists. It has also endangered his own grip on power by alienating Sunni Arabs and Kurds as well as raising hackles in the neighboring, predominantly Sunni, countries, especially Turkey and Saudi Arabia, who have come to see the Iraqi regime as a camp-follower of Iran and a supporter of the Assad regime in Syria. This could have deleterious consequences for the Iraqi regime if the Syrian regime is overthrown.

In Lebanon, Hizbullah, often characterized as a "terrorist" group in Western parlance – it would be more correct to refer to it as an Islamist resistance movement – has transformed itself quite successfully into a major political party, although it continues to possess an armed wing whose declared objective is to defend Lebanese territory and the Shia population of southern Lebanon against Israeli aggression. Since the end of the Lebanese civil war in 1990, with very few exceptions, Hizbullah has played by the confessional rules of Lebanese politics as enshrined in the Taif Agreement, which brought the civil war to a close. Only occasionally has it used its muscle power when it has felt its vital interests threatened, such as when the Sunni-dominated Lebanese government pushed it into a corner following the assassination of Rafiq Hariri in 2005.

Given its dual objectives since 1990 of militarily resisting Israeli domination and of representing the interests of the Shia of Lebanon as a normal political party, Hizbullah has had to take on a double role. On the one hand it acts as a well-organized political machine; on the other it refuses to disarm its armed wing as long as the Lebanese state is unable to protect its borders from Israeli intrusion. The Israeli invasion of Lebanon in 2006 proved Hizbullah's point that it was the sole defender of the country's sovereignty. The Lebanese forces took no part in the war, despite the heavy human and material damage inflicted on Lebanon by the Israeli invasion, which was projected as an Israel–Hizbullah conflict.

Hizbullah's relatively benign image in the Arab world, and more particularly the popularity of its leader Hassan Nasrallah, took a severe beating in 2013 with its increasingly open involvement in the Syrian civil war on behalf of the Assad regime. Hizbullah's strategic interests have dictated such a policy. These include the fact that Syria under Assad acts as the principal conduit for the passage of financial and arms aid from Iran, both of which are essential for Hizbullah to maintain its current position within Lebanon. Moreover, Iran is the principal supporter of both the Syrian regime and Hizbullah and has in all likelihood demanded that Hizbullah come to Assad's rescue as a quid pro quo for decades of Iranian military and financial assistance.

Nevertheless, Hizbullah's open military intervention in support of the Assad regime has damaged its credibility in much of the Arab world. It has also provided ammunition for those, such as Saudi Arabia, who would like to portray the battle for Syria as a Sunni–Shia struggle with Shia Iran and now Shia Hizbullah arrayed against the majority Sunni population of Syria and determined to deny the latter its legitimate rights. The Hizbullah case also determines the limits of Islamist power and popularity given the increasingly sectarian nature of Middle East politics and the dependence of some Islamist movements on outside support.

Whither Islamism?

These are, however, not the only constraints under which Islamist movements operate in the Middle East. Their slogan "Islam is the solution" may have worked as an effective way of mobilizing people against authoritarian regimes, but it does not provide the answer to the huge socio-economic problems faced by many countries in the region. Islamist parties in power are faced with the task of providing good governance and economic development within a participatory framework based upon societal consensus. It will not come as a surprise if these parties, who honed their political skills while in opposition, fail to rise to the task of governing societies with complex socio-economic problems that cannot be resolved in the short term, if at all. If this happens, the electorate is more than likely to throw them out of office in the next elections. The Islamist wave in the Arab Spring countries could then recede as quickly as it has advanced, returning these societies to a form of political equilibrium where power and popularity are more equally divided between Islamist and secular forces. The wave of mammoth demonstrations that eventually led to Egyptian President Morsi's ousting by the military clearly demonstrates the Egyptian public's disillusionment with the governing capacity and problem-solving capabilities of the Muslim Brotherhood. It could also be a signal that the tide of support for Islamist political parties is turning in the Middle East. However, the military coup against the Brotherhood government could have the opposite effect, of increasing sympathy for the Islamists in Egypt, especially if the military refuses to relinquish power quickly and continues its highly repressive policies, which have also begun to affect its civilian allies.

A major worry is that Morsi's departure by unconstitutional means has sent a signal to Islamist movements throughout the region that national and international forces will do their best to prevent them from governing even if they are elected in free and fair elections and have demonstrated their commitment to democratic constitutionalism. They may then conclude that the only way to gain and retain power is through the barrel of a gun. The Muslim Brotherhood had traveled a long way from the days of Syed Qutb but, unfortunately, current events in Egypt may be forcing Brotherhood members to re-read Qutb in the light of their present experiences and draw the most militant conclusions from his writings, as some of them did two decades earlier.

3

Deadlock over Palestine

Hamas is an Islamist movement but was not discussed in the last chapter because it is neither an opposition nor a governing Islamist party in the conventional sense of these terms. Nonetheless, it is a major protagonist in one of the longest-lasting conflicts in the Middle East, namely, that between Israel and Palestine. Hamas is an organization that combines nationalist and Islamist ideologies to fight foreign occupation politically and, sometimes, militarily. It has also acquired some governing functions in the Gaza Strip, but its attempt to rule over Gaza is severely circumscribed by Israel's blockade of the territory, periodic Israeli military invasions, and the intra-Palestinian rift between Hamas and Fatah that has divided Gaza from the Fatah-ruled West Bank.

Although officially established in 1987, at

the beginning of the first Palestinian *intifada* as the political arm of the Palestinian Muslim Brotherhood, Hamas is a product of the conflict over Palestine between Jewish colonizers and the indigenous Arab population going back to the 1920s and the beginnings of the British Mandate, which facilitated Jewish migration from Europe to Palestine. The Muslim Brotherhood has been active in Palestine since the 1930s and took part in the Great Palestinian Rebellion of 1936–9 against the British policy of Jewish colonization and the first war over Palestine against the Zionists in 1948.

After the occupation of the West Bank and Gaza in 1967, Israel itself provided the Palestinian Brotherhood social space to carry out its cultural and educational activities in the occupied territories. Israel facilitated this by turning a blind eye to, if not encouraging, the setting up of cultural and educational front organizations by the Brotherhood, which until the mid-1980s emphasized its educational and religious, and therefore apolitical, character, as an antidote to the nationalist and resistance activities in which the Palestine Liberation Organization (PLO) was engaged among Palestinians under occupation.[1] Israel believed that such a policy was likely to create divisions among the occupied population and would make its task as the occupier easier. Although the Brotherhood and the Fatah-led PLO were ideologically opposed to each other on many issues, it became clear by the mid-1980s that they shared the goal of liberating Palestine and that the Brotherhood had the capacity to turn itself into a political organization at short notice. The establishment of Hamas in 1987 to coincide with the first Palestinian *intifada* (uprising) proved this hypothesis correct.

At this point, it might be useful to pause briefly and consider the history of the unending Israel–Palestine conflict. While there is not space in this short book to explore its origins in detail, it is important to establish the fact that its root cause lies in the forcible demographic transformation of Palestine under the British Mandate, which lasted from 1922 until 1948. The British policy of encouraging and facilitating migration of European Jews into Palestine for a quarter-century, although implemented in fits and starts, was undertaken to fulfill the promise of establishing a Jewish homeland in Palestine made by London to the World Zionist Organization in the midst of World War I in the form of the Balfour Declaration of 1917. It dramatically changed the demographic map of Palestine by raising the Jewish share of the population from 11 percent in 1922 to 32 percent in

1947 and correspondingly decreasing the proportion of the indigenous Muslim and Christian Arab population.

Britain's post-World War I occupation of Palestine acted as the midwife for the colonization of Palestine by European Jews and the subsequent establishment of the State of Israel in 1948. This was determined by a vote of the then Euro-American-dominated UN General Assembly in November 1947 that, despite the opposition of all Arab and almost all Asian and African states who were members of the UN at that time, awarded the Jewish community in Palestine 55 percent of the country. Although the resolution partitioning Palestine, like all resolutions passed by the UN General Assembly, was merely recommendatory and not mandatory in character, Israel and its supporters constantly refer to it to justify Israel's legitimacy as a state in the heart of the Arab world.

Eventually Israel was established on 77 percent of the total land area of Palestine as a result of the armistice in 1949 between it and the neighboring Arab states who had intervened in the conflict. This war, described as the *nakba* (catastrophe) by the Palestinians, led to the expulsion of hundreds of thousands of Palestinian Arabs from their homes in what became Israel. A series of Arab–Israeli wars followed, leading to the occupation of the West Bank and Gaza by Israel in 1967, the continued Jewish settlement of occupied Palestinian territories, and the current stalemate that has fatally jeopardized the prospect of a two-state solution to the Israel–Palestine conflict.

The current situation in occupied Palestine has become untenable with a population that is chafing under a ruthless and wily occupation that continues to colonize what is left of Palestine while discussing the eventual dispensation of the occupied territories under a so-called "peace process" with a largely powerless Palestinian Authority (PA), whose leadership stands thoroughly discredited in the eyes of its own people. This led one astute observer to conclude, "[Israeli Prime Minister] Netanyahu is like a man who, while negotiating the division of a pizza, continues to eat it."[2] It should be noted that the colonization of occupied territories has been undertaken in direct violation of international law, especially the Fourth Geneva Convention, which prohibits the occupying power from transferring its own population to occupied lands thus changing the demographic character of these territories. It is estimated that currently there are over 350,000 Jewish settlers in the West Bank and another 300,000 in occupied East Jerusalem.[3]

Israel has been successful in expanding Jewish colonization of Palestinian territories, especially after the launching of the Oslo peace process in 1992, largely because of America's protective veto in the UN Security Council. Of the 83 vetoes cast by the United States at the UN Security Council, 58 have been cast on behalf of Israel. The American policy of vetoing, or threatening to veto, any and all resolutions critical of Israel's occupation policies has provided the latter the perfect cover to continue its illegal colonization of Palestinian territories.

It is in this context of increasing Palestinian despondency that Hamas emerged as the leading challenger to the Fatah-led PLO, the umbrella organization of Palestinian national movements that was founded in 1964 and became prominent beginning in the 1970s as the sole representative of the Palestinian people in the context of the conflict with Israel. The PLO, and its leading component Fatah, initially campaigned for the return of all of mandated Palestine to the Palestinians, but have since 1988 recognized Israel within its 1967 borders and limited their struggle to the liberation of the West Bank and Gaza from Israeli occupation. By contrast, Hamas has refused to recognize the legitimacy of the Israeli state and at least in theory is committed to liberating all of mandated Palestine from Zionist control.

Hamas's position as one of the two leading Palestinian political actors was confirmed by its victory over Fatah in the elections to the Palestinian Legislative Council in January 2006, in which it captured 76 of the 132 seats. It is now clear that no solution to the Israel–Palestine conflict is possible without its participation or at least consent. A series of shortsighted policies adopted both by the American administration and by Israel following Hamas's victory in 2006 deprived Hamas of the right to become the legitimate government in the Palestinian territories of Gaza and the West Bank. The United States insisted that Hamas had to immediately recognize the state of Israel, abjure violence, and drop its opposition to the Oslo peace process if it aspired to govern over the Palestinian territories, all of which run contrary to Hamas's stated position. Stringent economic sanctions imposed by the United States and Europe coupled with Israel's land and sea blockade of Gaza made it impossible for a Hamas government to attain power in Ramallah. Such policies also emboldened Fatah, which had received American financial aid to the tune of $2 million during its election campaign against Hamas, to deny the latter the legitimate fruits of its electoral victory.

A zero-sum game

It was clear from the very beginning that the American–Israeli reaction to Hamas's victory would be counterproductive. The very fact that in 2006 Hamas had participated in an election that was held under the Oslo framework – it had declined to do so in 1996 because it rejected the Oslo Accords – was indication enough of its willingness to eventually accept a two-state solution in one guise or another, as was its offer of a long-term *hudna* (truce) with Israel if the latter withdrew to the 1967 borders. Additionally, statements made by Hamas officials in the wake of its electoral victory implied that it was willing to prepare its constituency to accept a two-state solution in the long run.[4] Unfortunately, American and Israeli policies aborted an outcome that potentially offered a genuine opportunity for Hamas to mellow (and there were clear signs of such mellowing at the time of its electoral victory), thus augmenting the zero-sum trend that was already becoming visible in the Israel–Palestine conflict.

The American and Israeli refusal to engage with a Hamas-led PA emboldened Fatah to refuse to hand over power to Hamas, thus leading first to a stalemate and eventually in 2007 to Hamas taking control of Gaza by force and expelling PLO functionaries from the Strip. This amounted to the de facto partition of the occupied territories, with Hamas ruling over Gaza and Fatah continuing to govern the West Bank, both of course hemmed in by Israeli forces and Israeli control of access by land and sea to the occupied territories. Such a division of authority between the two Palestinian factions created another significant barrier to the launching of peace talks between Israel and the PA. It provided an additional excuse for Israeli foot-dragging on resuming peace talks since Israel refuses to engage in such talks with Hamas, and its preferred interlocutor, the PLO/PA, was not only unwilling until recently to renew negotiations as long as Israeli settlement activity continues but was also in no position to guarantee that any outcome will be acceptable to all segments of Palestinian society in the West Bank and Gaza.

However, principal responsibility for the continuing stalemate that has turned the Israel–Palestine conflict into a zero-sum game lies with a succession of Israeli governments that have expanded Jewish settlements in Palestinian territories and successfully carved up the occupied area into isolated Bantustans in such a fashion that there is little incentive left any longer for politically conscious Palestinians to support a two-state solution, regardless of the fact that it continues to be the PA's stated goal.

According to credible reports, 2011 was the record year in terms of Jewish settlement building in the West Bank and 2012 was the record year for building similar settlements in East Jerusalem, occupied by Israel in 1967.[5] This Israeli policy is a direct outcome of the fact that the occupied lands are a vital source of land and water for Israel and that continuing settlements satisfy a major political constituency in the country. This constituency consists of religious and non-religious ultra-nationalist Jews who consider the entire territory between the River Jordan and the Mediterranean Sea as part of Eretz Israel (Land of Israel). Since this constituency's participation is essential for building coalition governments in Israel, no Israeli government is likely to find itself in a position to trade land for peace as envisaged in the Oslo Accords.

The Israeli refusal to suspend settlement activity as a precondition for peace talks, which effectively shut the door on negotiations with the PA under Mahmoud Abbas, coincided with the Arab Spring, thus discrediting the Fatah-dominated PA at a critical time. It did so by bringing into sharper relief the issue of people's right to self-determination, freedom, and dignity, the major objectives of the democracy movements in the Arab world, all of which are denied to the Palestinians by the Israeli occupation. The Arab publics increasingly see Fatah and its auxiliary the PLO as Israel's collaborators in denying Palestinians these fundamental rights. The Israeli hard line has thus eroded the PA's credibility and redounded to the benefit of Hamas, which had been critical all along of PA President Abbas for his naïveté in putting his faith in negotiations with Israel to find a solution to the Israel–Palestine conflict, even when it had become clear that the so-called "peace process" was all process and no peace.

Thanks to the US Secretary of State John Kerry's relentless efforts, a new round of negotiations between Israel and the PA was launched in July 2013. However, this seemed directed more at deflecting criticism of the United States at the UN General Assembly session scheduled to meet in September 2013 for not pursuing the goal of a Palestinian state alongside Israel more actively than at reaching a final settlement of the dispute based on a viable two-state solution. At the same time, it served the purpose of buying more time for Israel to expand settlements in the occupied territories while warding off international criticism by engaging in negotiations that are bound to fail given its position on Jewish settlements and the status of Jerusalem.

It is worth noting that Israel's acceleration of Jewish colonization of the Palestinian territories was undertaken in clear defiance of the Obama administration's preferences. Netanyahu was able to successfully stare down the American President thanks to the strength of the Israeli lobby in Washington and its vice-like grip on both houses of the American Congress. This was demonstrated above all in May 2011 by the standing ovations Netanyahu received in the US Congress, which he addressed at the invitation of its Republican Speaker (not by invitation from the President, as is the tradition), when he made statements directly contradicting the United States' official stance on the Israel–Palestine conflict on a number of issues, including Jewish settlements and the status of Jerusalem.

It is a singular irony that Israel, which is by far the largest recipient of American largesse, has much greater clout in Washington than the United States has with Israeli policy-makers. It is estimated that since 1949 the United States has provided $115 billion in economic and military aid to Israel. American aid to Israel is currently estimated at $3 billion a year. Furthermore, America is the guarantor of Israel's qualitative military edge over all its Arab neighbors by providing it both with state-of-the-art weapon systems and with the most sophisticated weapons technology developed in the United States. All this is, of course, in addition to protecting Israel from condemnation in the UN Security Council that could potentially lead to sanctions similar to those imposed on countries, such as Iran and Syria and earlier Iraq and Libya, which repeatedly violate its resolutions.

Yet the tail continues to wag the dog – clear evidence of the influence of the Israeli lobby, especially of the American Israel Public Affairs Committee (AIPAC), which is dominated by Likud sympathizers who are far to the right of Jewish American mainstream opinion.[6] In 2013 this influential lobby almost scuttled Chuck Hagel's nomination by Obama to be Secretary of Defense in the US Senate because the nominee had on occasion mildly criticized Israeli policies and was perceived by Israel's friends in Congress, Republicans and Democrats alike, as not being hawkish enough on Iran's nuclear enrichment program, which Israel considers a threat to its security. It seems that given the mood within the Congress, henceforth the highest appointments to the President's national security team will have to be first approved by Israeli hawks before the US Senate confirms them.

It was in this context of prolonged stalemate

between Israel and the Palestinians – with the Israeli government bent on colonizing Palestinian lands at an accelerated pace; the PA refusing to negotiate with Israel unless and until settlement activity is stopped; and Hamas and Israel refusing to recognize each other as legitimate partners in the search for an Israeli–Palestinian peace – that democratic uprisings erupted in the Arab world from North Africa to the Fertile Crescent. These uprisings had the potential to impact at multiple levels the relationship between Israel and the Palestinians and the internal politics of the Palestinian territories, especially as they pertain to the balance between Hamas and Fatah. Much of this potential seems to have fizzled out as a result of the civil war in Syria and the military coup in Egypt that deposed the elected government, whose sympathies clearly lay with Hamas both in the latter's resistance to Israeli occupation and in its relations with Fatah.

The impact of the Arab uprisings

The major immediate impact of the Arab uprisings on the Israel–Palestine equation resulted from the removal of the Mubarak regime in Egypt and its replacement by a democratically elected government led by the Muslim Brotherhood, which was subsequently overthrown by the Egyptian military in July 2013. This did not mean that the Morsi government was in a position to fundamentally reverse course in its policy toward Israel. It remained committed to the Egyptian–Israeli Peace Treaty for two principal reasons. First, the Egyptian military, aware of its inferiority in terms of weapons systems and its dependence on the United States for advanced weaponry and financial subsidies, was both unable and unwilling to adopt a militarily hostile posture vis-à-vis Israel that might escalate into a full-fledged war. Second, the civilian government was equally aware of its financial dependence on the United States and on the international lending agencies that are dominated by America and its allies. It was also fully cognizant of the fact that American financial and military transfers were directly dependent upon its upholding the peace treaty with Israel and that they were likely to be abruptly cut off if Cairo adopted a hostile posture toward the Jewish state. Therefore, there was little chance that Egypt, even under a Brotherhood government, would formally renege on the peace treaty with Israel.

However, there were perceptible shifts in Cairo's attitude toward Hamas-ruled Gaza and in the atmospherics surrounding Egypt's relations with

Israel. There were two major reasons for this shift. First, Egyptian public opinion is markedly anti-Israel, and this was bound to be reflected in the attitude of any popularly elected government. A 2012 Pew Research Center Global Attitudes Project poll concluded that Egyptians would like to annul the peace treaty with Israel by a ratio of almost 2 to 1.[7] Simultaneously, the University of Maryland's annual survey of public opinion in Egypt indicated that 94 percent of Egyptians considered Israel to be one of the two countries posing the biggest threat to their country; the other was the United States, which was identified as a threat by 80 percent of the respondents.[8]

Second, the Egyptian Muslim Brotherhood has close ideological affinity with the Palestinian Muslim Brotherhood. Hamas, currently in control of Gaza, which is contiguous to Egypt, is, as noted above, the political arm of the Palestinian Muslim Brotherhood. Given the hostility between Hamas and Israel, the occasional exchange of fire between the two, and eventually the air offensive launched by Israel against Gaza in November 2012, the Egyptian Muslim Brotherhood would have been hard put to justify its commitment to unconditional peaceful relations with Israel before its own constituency. While President Morsi acted as a mediator between Hamas and Israel and thus helped bring the November 2012 conflict to a close, it would have been extremely difficult for the Brotherhood to justify a policy of equidistance between Hamas and Israel in future crises between the two antagonists.

Furthermore, any popularly elected government in Egypt would be unlikely to squeeze the Hamas authorities in Gaza by imposing a de facto blockade on them in tandem with Israel the way the Mubarak regime had done between 2007 and 2011. While a civilian government may be reluctant to allow a full-fledged re-arming of Hamas through tunnels linking Egypt to Gaza, it is likely to allow some military hardware to pass into Hamas's hands through Egypt in addition to goods needed for humanitarian and civilian purposes. It will be forced to do so to maintain some degree of credibility with the Egyptian population. This explains why Israel has so forcefully backed the military coup in Egypt and has lobbied hard in Washington to protect the military-installed government from the negative consequences of the army's overthrow of an elected government. The Egyptian military, with whom its Israeli counterpart has been dealing for decades, is undoubtedly Israel's favorite constituency in that country.

However, no government in Cairo may be in a position to put an end completely to the smuggling, including arms traffic, which goes on through the 400 or so tunnels under the 14.5 kilometer border between Sinai and the Gaza Strip. Declining state authority following the collapse of the Mubarak regime has not only benefited smugglers but also permitted the infiltration of al-Qaeda-linked extremists into the region. This has further complicated Egypt's relations both with Israel and with Hamas since these extremists not only have their own anti-Israeli agenda but they also consider Hamas to be too moderate and compromising in its dealings with the Jewish state and are interested in the further radicalization of Hamas-controlled Gaza.

Initially, the Arab Spring also threatened to change the balance between Hamas and Fatah in the occupied Palestinian territories. Hamas traded one principal supporter, Syria, for another, Egypt, as long as the Muslim Brotherhood was in power in Cairo. The violence that engulfed Syria from the middle of 2011, the involvement of the Syrian Muslim Brotherhood, an ideological sibling of Hamas, as a leading participant in the anti-Assad movement, and the overall Palestinian sympathy for the democratic movement in Syria forced Hamas to distance itself from Assad and remove its headquarters in exile from Damascus. Khaled Meshal, head of the Hamas Politburo, who had lived in exile in Syria for several years, left Damascus for Qatar in January 2012. Hamas's break with Syria reached its culmination with the stinging denunciation of the Assad regime and vocal support for the Syrian democratic movement by Hamas's Prime Minister of Gaza, Ismail Haniyah, in a notable speech delivered at the famous Al-Azhar mosque in Cairo in February 2012. He did so partly as a consequence of unbearable pressure put upon the exiled leadership by the Assad regime to come out in the latter's support against the regime's opponents.

Denouncing the Assad regime and closing its Syrian base was a radical departure for Hamas since it had prided itself on being a part of the resistance front against Israel with Syria, Iran, and the Lebanese Hizbullah as its other members. Qatar, but more particularly its anti-Assad ally Saudi Arabia, is seen as a supporter of the Fatah-led PLO as well as hostile to Iran, the Syrian regime's main ally in the region. Hamas's decision to move its exile headquarters to Qatar, therefore, signaled not only a break with Syria but also a possible downgrading of its relations with Iran, which has supported the movement not only politically but also financially and militarily.

However, initially Hamas made up for these losses, at least in part, by the change of government in Egypt that brought the Muslim Brotherhood to power next door to Gaza. It is true that the Muslim Brotherhood, as stated earlier, had to perform a deft balancing act between its ideological affinities and Egyptian popular sympathies for Hamas, on the one hand, and its commitment to the peace treaty with Israel and its need for American aid, on the other. Nonetheless, it was clear that the Egyptian government's sympathies lay with Hamas as long as President Morsi and the Brotherhood remained in office. This situation changed dramatically with the military coup of July 2013, which has led not only to the closing of borders between Egypt and Gaza but also to the Egyptian government blocking off most of the trade through the underground tunnels connecting Gaza with Egypt, thus cutting off the former's economic lifeline. People's movements between Gaza and Egypt have also been drastically curtailed, thereby adding immensely to the humanitarian crisis already facing the Gaza population. The situation seems to have more or less returned to the days of the Mubarak regime with Gaza once again under siege by both Israel and Egypt.

Both the coming to power of the Brotherhood-dominated elected government and its removal by military force affected the equation between Hamas and Fatah as well. Whereas under Mubarak the Egyptian government was openly supportive of Fatah against Hamas, the Morsi government had adopted an even-handed approach between the two and began to act as a genuine facilitator for Palestinian unity talks between the rival factions. The last round of such talks was held in Cairo in January 2013. The escalating political crisis in Cairo leading to the coup has prevented the reconvening of the intra-Palestinian talks. Not much progress has been made toward the unification of the West Bank and Gaza so far. Prospects for any movement on this issue are dim because it is reasonable to assume that Egypt will once again return to a more pro-Fatah stance under the military-dominated regime. Indications that this is happening are provided by the fact that the military-installed regime and the government-controlled press have harshly criticized Hamas for interfering in Egyptian domestic affairs by allegedly extending support to Morsi's followers after his overthrow. Moreover, given the fact that the current Egyptian government is heavily dependent upon Saudi Arabia and its Gulf allies, especially Kuwait and the United Arab Emirates, for economic sustenance, it is bound to follow the Saudi lead in supporting Fatah and shunning

Hamas, which as an offshoot of the Brotherhood is anathema to Riyadh.

The ouster of Mubarak had come as a big blow to Fatah and the return of the military to power in Egypt has provided it some respite by increasing the economic and political pressure on Hamas, which has lost two friends, Syria and Egypt, in quick succession. However, it does not solve Fatah's basic dilemma, for the PA, which it dominates, is perceived by most Palestinians not only as weak vis-à-vis Israel but, in fact, as an agent of Israeli control over the restive population of the West Bank. This image is augmented by the PA's financial dependence on Israel, which acts as its customs duties collector and also permits – and sometimes withholds – the passage of funds from other sources to the PA. Moreover, the PA's security forces coordinate their activities with their Israeli counterparts in an effort to keep the Palestinian population of the West Bank under control. Consequently, all that the PA can do vis-à-vis Israel is plead and not defy.

However, the PA's attitude toward Israel does not reflect the Palestinian reality on the ground. As prospects for a negotiated settlement of the conflict have receded and as Palestinian frustration with the peace process and continuing Jewish colonization has multiplied, there are indications that a third Palestinian *intifada* on the West Bank is likely to erupt, catching both the PA and Israel off-guard. Democracy uprisings in the rest of the Arab world, as well as Hamas's defiance of Israel during the November 2012 conflict, which ended in a stalemate despite Israel's tremendous military superiority and its control of Gaza's airspace, are likely to encourage another Palestinian uprising in the West Bank, which has remained relatively quiet for more than ten years. Such an uprising, which is likely to have both non-violent and violent dimensions, could trigger another shooting war between Hamas-controlled Gaza and Israel as well, thus throwing the entire region into greater turmoil and this time forcing Arab regimes, above all Egypt and Jordan, to choose sides, however reluctant they may be to do so.

Any event such as the death of a Palestinian prisoner in Israeli custody or the shooting of a Palestinian teenager throwing stones at Israeli soldiers could act as a spark igniting the third *intifada* because the kindling is already present in ample measure. Given the fact that the Fatah-dominated PA is increasingly seen not as a deliverer of the State of Palestine but as Israel's security agent in the West Bank, the next *intifada* is likely to target the PA as well as Israel, and this could redound to Hamas's benefit. It is clear that PLO President Mahmoud

Abbas and his government, which has lost two Prime Ministers in quick succession, is at a dead end and unable to chart a clear policy toward either Israel or Hamas.

As we have seen, the Arab uprisings and changes in the regional environment had to some extent energized both Hamas and Fatah to engage in negotiations mediated by Egypt about the unification of Gaza and the West Bank as well as Hamas's admission into the PLO, the umbrella organization of Palestinian groups that includes all factions except Hamas. These negotiations have been inconclusive so far because both parties are reluctant to give up exclusive power over the territories they control. Although there has been some relaxation of the ban on Hamas's public activities in the West Bank and similar Fatah activities in Gaza, such steps have not resulted in any concrete move toward the reunification of the two parts of occupied Palestine. However, it seems to be increasingly clear that time is not on the side of Fatah, despite the current problems faced by its rival Hamas. Fatah has progressively lost ground to Hamas before the bar of Palestinian and Arab public opinion. Consequently, Israel and the United States may soon be faced with a situation where they will either have to negotiate directly with Hamas in order to bring the

Israel–Palestine conflict to a close or have to face the prospect of a massive outburst of revolt in the West Bank with a corresponding downward spiral into conflict between Israel and Gaza. The fuse seems to be getting shorter all the time.

The end of the two-state solution

Time is not on the side of a two-state solution either. It is becoming ever more apparent that such a solution may have lost its allure for Palestinians and Israelis alike. With Israeli opinion turning increasingly rightward and the old Fatah guard, above all Mahmoud Abbas, about to pass from the scene, the prospect for a Palestinian state alongside Israel is receding fast. The Israeli Economy Minister, Naftali Bennet, who heads the hardline nationalist Jewish Home Party, bluntly summed up the dominant opinion within the current Israeli government in the following words: "The idea that a Palestinian state will be founded within the Land of Israel has reached a dead-end. . . . Never, in the history of Israel, have so many people put so much energy into something so pointless. . . . The most important thing for the Land of Israel is to build, and build, and build [Jewish settlements]."[9]

Such views, which have been gaining ground within Israel, and more particularly within the Israeli government, open up frightening possibilities of civil war in the entire area comprising Israel and the occupied Palestinian territories. The bottom line seems to be becoming increasingly clear: whatever its character, there is likely to be only one state in what used to be British mandatory Palestine. The chances are that this state will be based on a relationship of Jewish superiority and Palestinian inferiority, in other words, apartheid. This is expected to be the case because the granting of equal political and civil rights to all its citizens would mean that the state, even if it continues to be called Israel, will lose its exclusivist Jewish character, thus reversing Zionist goals and achievements – an outcome that will not be acceptable to the large majority of Israel's Jewish population.

An apartheid state such as the one envisaged above, which in all probability will be the end result of the present trajectory of Israeli policies, will be a sure recipe for perpetual conflict between the two nations inhabiting the territory between the River Jordan and the Mediterranean Sea. This is likely to be accompanied by international opprobrium as well as global ostracism of Israel – an outcome that even the United States will be unable to prevent despite its veto power in the UN Security Council. What is more, conflict within a bi-national but apartheid Israel is bound to spill over its borders, triggering off one or a series of major regional conflagrations. If this scenario unfolds, and given Israel's adamant refusal to halt the Jewish colonization of Palestinian lands it is likely to do so, then the Middle East would have taken a giant step toward implosion. This can be expected to have extremely deleterious consequences for the United States and other Western powers that have major strategic and economic interests in the region since they are seen in the Middle East as supporters and friends of Israel and, therefore, legitimate targets of Arab anger.

4

Regional and Global Rivalries

The Israel–Palestine conflict has a life of its own independent of the Arab Spring. In contrast, the connection between the recent upheavals in the Arab world and escalating rivalry among regional and global powers in the Middle East is more direct and easy to discern. The uprisings in individual Arab countries emanated from discrete domestic contexts of political repression, economic stagnation, and denial of civil rights. However, their outcomes were and continue to be strongly influenced, if not determined, by the broader regional and global settings, especially the actions and reactions of major regional powers as well as of extra-regional powers with important strategic and economic interests in the Middle East.

Military and political stalemate in Syria; the aborting of the democratic movement in Bahrain;

uncertainty about the future of Yemen; the chaotic and indecisive nature of the Libyan transition; the military coup in Egypt leading to the overthrow of the elected government – all have been influenced to different degrees by the stands adopted by regional and global powers and, quite often, by their intervention in the process of transition. Consequently, in several cases the autonomous domestic dynamics of political change have been subverted by the intrusion of external powers with their own objectives and agendas often distinct from those of domestic political actors.

The Arab Spring was never the autonomous phenomenon most people were led to believe during its initial phase when Tunisia and Egypt seemed to be leading the way toward a democratic future for the region. The suppression of the Bahraini movement for democracy, the external manipulation of the outcome in Yemen, which, despite some hopeful signs, remains unsettled, and the Libyan civil war were indications that the process was far from immune from external involvement. The insurgency in Syria, which has been transformed into a bloody civil war by external intervention on both sides of the political divide, has laid to rest any lingering doubts that major external players, with their own interests and objectives, have the capability to make or mar outcomes of the Arab uprisings.

One cannot, therefore, establish a complete picture of the Arab uprisings and their likely outcomes without taking into account the interests, policies, and political and military interventions undertaken by outside powers that have often exacerbated domestic conflicts and immensely complicated the process of transition to democratic and open societies. These external intrusions have in several cases transformed national uprisings into potential regional conflicts, some of which could have significant global ramifications. Let us look at these carefully in turn.

Egypt

Yemen, Libya, Bahrain, and Syria clearly testify to the importance of external involvement in anti-regime uprisings in the Arab world. In all these cases foreign intervention shaped the course of events to an equal or greater extent compared with local forces engaged in the struggle for defending regimes or transforming them. But even in the case of Egypt, where it appeared that internal dynamics, the Tahrir demonstrations, were primarily responsible for the overthrow of the Mubarak dictatorship, all eyes were focused on Washington throughout the anti-Mubarak protests, despite the fact that it was clear that the American administration had been caught unawares by the Egyptian uprising. It was evident to discerning observers that Mubarak would not have fallen as quickly and completely had Washington not been loath to intervene to save his regime.

It was also clear that, following the overthrow of Mubarak, leaders of major political organizations, especially the Muslim Brotherhood, which emerged as the leading political force, were keenly aware of American, Saudi, and Israeli interests and how they might affect the future of Egypt. American military aid had amounted to $1.3 billion a year since 1987 and was both a quid pro quo for Egypt's peace treaty with Israel and aimed at shoring up Mubarak's authoritarian regime. It was essential for the post-Mubarak government to keep this aid flowing lest its cessation lead to military disgruntlement boiling over and threatening the existence of the elected government – a strategy that eventually failed to prevent its ouster by a military coup.

Similarly, Saudi Arabia provided over $2 billion in aid to Egypt while SCAF (the Supreme Command of the Armed Forces), the post-Mubarak military junta, was in power, and it was widely reported that Riyadh was in favor of continued military rule in Egypt – a conclusion that was vindicated by the Saudi regime's whole-hearted support of the military coup of July 2013. There were two primary reasons for Riyadh's antipathy toward democratic change in Egypt. One, it did not want the revolutionary contagion to spread beyond Egypt and believed that the Egyptian military would be able to keep the revolutionaries on a tight leash or, even better, abort the democratic process. Two, it was opposed to a Muslim Brotherhood government taking power in Cairo because of its hostility toward the message of the party, which uses Islamic rhetoric for popular political mobilization, especially against authoritarian regimes. This is perceived by Riyadh as a major threat to the Saudi political system, which draws its legitimacy from its "Islamic" credentials but uses Islam to instill political docility and unquestioning loyalty to the House of Saud among its subjects. As stated above, it was no coincidence that Saudi Arabia was the first country to endorse the anti-Morsi coup, with the Saudi monarch personally congratulating the military-appointed interim President Adly Mansour, a holdover from the Mubarak regime.

Despite the fundamental ideological differences between the Muslim Brotherhood and the Saudi regime, Egypt's economic dependence on Saudi Arabia, especially in terms of oil supply at concessional rates and financial repatriation by Egyptians working in the Kingdom in large numbers, forced the Morsi government to keep the Saudi regime in good humor. In return, Saudi Arabia and the gas-rich tiny kingdom of Qatar poured cash, reportedly amounting to about $14 billion, into the Egyptian coffers.[1] It is difficult to know how much of this aid reached Egypt before Morsi's ouster but it was clear that it was aimed at preventing Egypt going bankrupt, thus leading to further unrest acting as a prelude to the intensification of anti-regime movements in Arab countries that have so far remained immune to the revolutionary contagion.

Major constraints were also visible in Egypt's relations with Israel under the Morsi presidency as maintaining the Egyptian–Israeli Peace Treaty is an integral part of the political and financial bargain Cairo has struck with Washington since the time of Anwar Sadat. This is clear from the fact, as discussed in chapter 3, that the Brotherhood-dominated government had to tread a fine line between its ideological affinity and Egyptian popular support for Hamas in control of Gaza, on the one hand, and the need not to alienate Israel to a point that it may affect the American–Egyptian relationship, on the other. The Morsi government's frantic attempt to broker a cease-fire between Israel and Hamas in November 2012 was dictated primarily by its apprehension that if Israel launched a ground invasion of Gaza, Egyptian public opinion was likely to force it to adopt anti-Israeli postures, not excluding at least a symbolic suspension of the Peace Treaty, that would impact negatively on Cairo's relations with Washington. However, the Brotherhood's cautionary policy did not cut much ice with the Israeli government, which welcomed the military coup of July 2013 as it has traditionally had a far better working relationship with the Egyptian military and intelligence officials in the past and considers the military to be far less sympathetic, in fact hostile, to Hamas.

The United States seemed to be fully aware of the constraints that such dependencies imposed upon the Muslim Brotherhood's behavior and the latter's willingness to work within these constraints. There have been credible reports in the wake of the coup that the United States tried to intervene to work out a compromise between Morsi and the army-supported opposition before the coup and has been trying to coax the Brotherhood to accept the fait accompli and reconcile itself to the new dispensation.[2] However, Washington has been reluctant to term the military takeover a coup because it could negatively impact American military and economic assistance to Egypt under American law. US Secretary of State Kerry has, in fact, gone to the extent of characterizing the coup as a step toward the "restoration of democracy" in Egypt, despite the massacre of almost a thousand Muslim Brotherhood supporters by the security services and the internment of the organization's top leadership in the wake of Morsi's ouster. It appears that, like Israel, the US administration feels more comfortable working with a military-installed government than with an elected Egyptian leadership that would be amenable to the pressure of public opinion and, therefore, critical of America.

Yemen

If external factors influenced the transformation of the Egyptian regime, the outcome of its uprising, and the legitimization of the July 2013 military takeover in subtle ways, their impact on the process of regime change in Yemen has been more clearly visible. This is a continuation of Yemen's vulnerability to foreign interference and is largely a function of domestic instability and internal conflict that has pervaded the country during the past two decades following the unity agreement between South and North Yemen that established a single Yemeni state in 1990. Significant elements in South Yemen never really reconciled themselves to a union dominated by the northern elite centered in the capital Sanaa. The increasing concentration of power in the hands of Ali Abdullah Saleh, who had ruled North Yemen since 1978, became President of the united country in 1990, and used harsh force to quell the opposition, further exacerbated inter-regional antagonisms within Yemen and led to a civil war in 1994 that was won by the north but left the defeated south in a sullen mood. The two decades since that civil war have continued to reflect the enduring regional fragmentation and tribal divisions in Yemen, thus facilitating intervention by outside powers with strategic and economic interests in the country.[3]

Foreign interference, in turn, has played no small role in exacerbating regional, tribal, and sectarian divisions in Yemen. Above all, Saudi Arabia has been involved in Yemeni affairs for decades. In the 1960s it provided arms and money to royalist forces fighting Egyptian-backed Arab nationalist military officers who had staged a coup, deposed the Imam of Yemen, and established a republic. It has continued to support conservative tribal and religious leaders more recently, while at the same time supporting Saleh's authoritarian regime, often at odds with these same elements.

The United States has been involved in Yemeni affairs especially since the bombing of the USS *Cole* in 2000 by al-Qaeda-linked operatives. Washington supported the Saleh regime, which it considered to be a partner in the fight against al-Qaeda, and Saleh did indeed provide Washington great latitude in hunting down al-Qaeda operatives through remotely piloted drones and by other means. Paradoxically, given the anarchical conditions prevailing in the country and America's increasing unpopularity among Yemenis because of its drone attacks that have led to civilian casualties, Yemen has become the primary base of AQAP (Al-Qaeda in the Arabian Peninsula) during the past ten years after its leadership was decimated in Saudi Arabia or forced to flee to the neighboring country.

However, both Saudi Arabia and the United States were caught flat-footed when the democracy movement gained momentum in the capital Sanaa in 2011 following the overthrow of Mubarak in Egypt. In fact, parts of the country had been engaged in open rebellion against the government since 2007, but this had been overshadowed in Western accounts by Yemen's role in the overall American strategy of decimating the al-Qaeda leadership based there, which seemed to pose the greatest terrorist threat to the United States following the defeat and liquidation of the organization's central leadership in the wake of the American invasion of Afghanistan in 2001–2.[4] Although the democracy movement in Sanaa in 2011 seemed to superficially mirror the movements in Tunis and Cairo, given the fractured nature of the country and its elite the movement soon became intertwined with tribal rebellions and military revolts. This became very clear once Saleh's grip began to slip and a free for all ensued in Yemen, with the capital itself threatened by anarchy.

When it became obvious that Saleh had become an unmitigated liability for them, the Saudis and the Americans brokered a transfer of power to his Vice-President, Abd Rabu Mansur Hadi, under a formula that provided amnesty to Saleh and his family. This has allowed the latter the freedom to continue to engage in disruptive politics in Yemen, among other things by defying Hadi's orders even after he was elected President unopposed in February 2012. Recent reports suggest that Hadi may have had some success in sidelining Saleh's sons and nephews in an overhaul of the military command, but the jury is still out on this issue.

At the same time, secessionist forces have gained strength in the south, and the Shia Zaidi rebellion in the north, now known as the Houthi movement, has picked up steam, reportedly with the help of Iran, motivated by its animus against Saudi Arabia and the United States. Saudi and American involvement, goaded both by Saudi–Iranian rivalry and by the United States' war against al-Qaeda, exacerbated the anarchical situation in Yemen, first by perpetuating Saleh's rule and then by overseeing a power transition that has left behind much of the malaise that had plagued the country under the dictatorial regime. The transition to democracy has been severely curtailed if not aborted by the actions of outside powers.

Libya

In Libya, foreign intervention was not merely transparent; it was decisive in bringing about regime change. While the Yemeni transition has been brokered by external powers, the overthrow of the Qaddafi regime in Libya would not have been possible as quickly as it happened, if at all, without the help of NATO's airpower and British and French advisors on the ground training and advising the militias fighting government forces. In fact, it has been argued that in the initial stages of the rebellion, when Qaddafi's forces put up stiff resistance against the insurgents centered in Benghazi in the east, NATO's intervention saved the latter from defeat.[5]

The speed with which the UN Security Council, NATO, and the United States acted to impose a no-fly zone apparently for humanitarian reasons and then under this guise decimated Qaddafi's forces from the air was indeed astonishing. It was remarkable because a lengthy and often tortuous process of negotiation and bargaining normally precedes international intervention even in cases of impending humanitarian crises such as those in Rwanda and Bosnia. In this case, the UN Security Council adopted a resolution authorizing the establishment of a no-fly zone over Libya as well as "all necessary measures" to protect the civilian population within five weeks of the beginning of the demonstrations against Qaddafi's rule. More significantly, France, Britain, and the United States launched military strikes within a couple of days of the passage of the resolution. NATO began to act as the air arm of the Libyan rebellion soon thereafter.

There was also a remarkable degree of consensus among members of the Arab League that Qaddafi had to be removed. It was a testimony to his unpopularity among his fellow-Arab rulers that the Arab League quickly passed a resolution demanding international intervention for his ouster. Qatar and the United Arab Emirates were at the forefront of this campaign with support from Saudi Arabia. Qatar was the first country to recognize the National Transitional Council on March 28, 2011, as the sole, legitimate representative of the Libyan people. Turkey, which had been initially reluctant to intervene, also jumped on the bandwagon once it became clear that NATO was committed not only to intervening in the Libyan civil war but also to bringing it to a successful conclusion.

Why were the NATO powers and the Arab states of the Persian Gulf so enthusiastic about intervening in Libya? For a start, the uprising in the country was much more violent than in Tunisia or Egypt and both sides engaged in military action almost from the very beginning. The two parties also seemed to be quite evenly matched, thus presenting the alarming prospect of a mounting death toll as the conflict was prolonged indefinitely, which was likely to be the case without external intervention.

Such an outcome could have resulted in a humanitarian disaster. More important in galvanizing NATO intervention, such a humanitarian crisis also threatened European economic and strategic interests in Libya, especially renewed investments in the exploration and extraction of oil, and also portended a flood of refugees, both Libyans and foreign, especially sub-Saharan African, workers employed in the country or working for Qaddafi's security agencies. Moreover, given the remarkable consensus both among the major powers and among the Arab states as to who were the good guys and who were the bad guys in Libya, there seemed little prospect of hostile international reaction if NATO, covered by UN Security Council Resolution 1973, intervened militarily on behalf of the anti-Qaddafi forces.

Russia and China abstained but did not block the Security Council resolution, which established a no-fly zone over Libya and imposed an arms embargo on the Libyan government. However, they learnt the lesson from the Libyan case not to repeat this mistake because the Western powers interpreted the UN mandate very liberally, turning a humanitarian mission into one directed at regime change. Consequently, Moscow and Beijing are adamant about not allowing the Security Council to sanction any form of intervention in the civil war in Syria because they are convinced that the Western powers will subvert the original intent of the resolution to suit their own objective of overthrowing the Assad regime. This may not prevent the Western powers, especially the United States, from taking military action against the Assad government, but it will deny such use of force the international legitimacy that only a UN Security Council resolution can provide.

Strategic importance and external intervention

While Libya is a good case study of externally driven regime change in the Arab world, Syria and Bahrain provide the two most strategically important cases of external intervention in the process of domestically initiated attempts to achieve democratic change. The reason for this is two-fold: firstly, both have become battlegrounds where the regional cold war between Saudi Arabia and Iran for pre-eminence in the Persian Gulf and the broader Middle East is taking place; secondly, both countries host important overseas bases of global powers. Bahrain, as noted in chapter 2, is the head-quarters of the US Fifth Fleet, which is responsible for American naval forces in the Persian Gulf, Red Sea, Arabian Sea, and the East African coast as far south as Kenya. The military significance of the Fifth Fleet has been greatly enhanced because of the confrontation between the United States and Iran on the issue of Iran's nuclear enrichment program. The Fifth Fleet's armada will be in charge of carrying out any decision by Washington to launch strikes against Iranian nuclear facilities. Syria hosts Russia's only overseas military base outside of the former Soviet space and its only military outpost in the Mediterranean. The Tartus base's psychological significance for Moscow exceeds its strategic value as it gives Russia a feeling that it is still a great power with global reach.

Who wins in Bahrain and Syria is therefore of considerable importance both to regional and to global powers, and this explains the high degree of external involvement in both cases. Consequently, such intervention has significantly affected outcomes in both countries, with Syria mired in a civil war and headed toward anarchy and state failure and the democratic movement in Bahrain all but crushed by the use of overwhelming force encouraged and assisted by Saudi Arabia with what appears to be the blessings of the United States.

Syria

Syria has for many decades been the bellwether of Arab politics, especially in times of intense ideological competition. It was seen as the ultimate prize for contending trends and powers throughout much of the twentieth century; whichever ideological or political tendency emerged victorious in Syria came to dominate, more often than not, the Arab political scene. This was true in the 1950s and 1960s during the time of intense competition, indeed an Arab cold war, between "revolutionary" military regimes espousing the cause of Arab nationalism and conservative monarchies determined to hold on to their power and privilege with the assistance of their Western allies.[6]

However, this time around, non-Arab Iran is a leading protagonist in the new cold war in the Middle East, with Saudi Arabia as the rival pole of power. Also, the competition is ideologically blurred, especially in the case of Syria where arch-conservative Gulf monarchies that consider democracy anathema are ostensibly supporting the cause of democracy while the authoritarian Assad regime has the support of Iran, whose hybrid political system encompasses both clerical and representative institutions. Democratic Turkey's involvement in Syria has complicated the picture further, with Ankara and Riyadh, strange bed-fellows to say the least, lined up on the side of the opposition and Iran on the side of the regime. Once you throw into this mix the global rivalry between Washington and Moscow, both of whom are involved in the Syrian conflict, the country emerges as the quintessential battleground where several proxy wars are being fought simultaneously.

It is often argued that Iran's role in the current regional cold war has introduced sectarian (Shia versus Sunni) as well as ethnic (Persian versus Arab) divisions into the competition for pre-eminence in the region. But to be fair to Tehran, its support for the Assad regime is primarily driven by strategic rather than sectarian (leave alone ethnic) considerations. Tehran is a firm supporter of the Assad regime because the latter was its only loyal Arab ally during the dark days of the eight-year war imposed on Iran by Iraq when all other Arab governments, principally the Gulf monarchies newly flush with petro-dollars, not only supported Iraq but largely financed Saddam's war machine. Equally, or more, important, Syria has been from the 1980s the principal conduit for Iranian military and financial assistance to the Lebanese Hizbullah and until recently to the Palestinian Hamas.

Additionally, Syria under Assad is perceived by the Iranian regime as a part of the "resistance" front against Israel, one of Iran's two primary regional antagonists – the other being Saudi Arabia. It is the authoritarian Sunni Arab regimes, such as those in Saudi Arabia and Jordan (and until 2011 Egypt under Mubarak), that fanned the fires of sectarian conflict by dubbing Iran's support to the Alawite-dominated regime in Syria sectarian and part of the Iranian effort to create a Shia crescent in order to dominate the Middle East. The charge of sectarianism makes little sense since the Alawites who dominate the Syrian regime are considered at best heretics and at worst non-Muslim by most Muslims, Sunni and Shia alike. However, the charge has gained a degree of credibility because most people outside the Muslim world consider Alawites to be Shia and this narrative fits in with the Shia-dominated Iraqi government's close relationship with the Iranian regime and Shia Hizbullah's dependence upon Iran for military and financial support.

Two recent events have added to the strength of the argument that Iran is committed to establishing a predominantly Shia zone of influence in the Arab world. Firstly, since 2013, battle-hardened Hizbullah troops have entered the fray in Syria, probably at the instance of Tehran, to bolster the Assad regime's military capabilities, and this has made a measurable difference to the balance of forces on the ground. Secondly, the al-Maliki government in Iraq has clandestinely provided Iran overflight facilities for transporting weapons to the Syrian government forces, thus adding to the regime's military capabilities.

Iran's policy toward the Syrian conflict can be best explained by the fact that while the overthrow of Saddam Hussein opened up major opportunities for Iran to gain influence in Iraq, continuing uncertainties in that country, including prospects of renewed sectarian conflict and the unstable nature of the Shia-dominated governments in Baghdad, make Syria a strategic asset for Iran that it cannot readily sacrifice. For the Assad regime, Iran is a source of military aid as well as financial assistance. Given the current distribution of power and influence in the Middle East, Tehran and Damascus need each other.

It is also worth noting that Iran's policy toward both Iraq and Hizbullah is only partly driven by sectarian-religious considerations. Tehran considers it essential to have a friendly regime in Baghdad because it cannot afford the colossal damage that renewed war with Iraq would entail, as happened between 1980 and 1988 when Saddam Hussein was in power. The empowerment of the Shia majority in Iraq in the wake of Saddam's fall contributes to Iran's sense of security vis-à-vis its neighbor, especially because all the major Shia parties in Iraq are led by people beholden to Iran, which gave them refuge and trained their militias during Saddam's rule.

The Lebanese Hizbullah has had close religious and ideological affinity with the ruling clerical elements in Iran from its very founding. Nonetheless, the relationship has a strategic logic as well – Hizbullah is the only Arab force that has demonstrated that it is capable of standing up to Israel and giving it a bloody nose, as it did during the Israeli invasion of Lebanon in 2006. Hizbullah's military capabilities provide Iran a backdoor option against Israel in case of an Israeli or Israeli–American attack on Iran's nuclear facilities.

Conversely, Saudi Arabia, engaged in a tussle for pre-eminence with Iran in the Persian Gulf, supports the Sunni-dominated opposition against the Assad regime, again not so much for sectarian reasons, although it publicly emphasizes the sectarian aspect to discredit the Assad regime in the eyes of the predominantly Sunni Arab publics, but because of the Syrian regime's connection with

Iran. For the Saudis and their monarchical allies in the Persian Gulf, keeping Iran bogged down in the Syrian quagmire diverts Tehran's attention and capabilities from the Gulf theater, thus benefiting the Arab kingdoms already apprehensive of the fall-out of the Arab Spring on their own legitimacy and longevity. The uprising in Bahrain, brutally crushed by the al-Khalifa regime with military support from Saudi Arabia, has made the absolute rulers of the Gulf very nervous about their own future. This has led to their campaign to paint the democracy movement in Bahrain as an Iranian conspiracy in order to gain the support of the Arab publics and the Western powers.

Saudi Arabia and Qatar have not only extended financial support to the Syrian opposition but in conjunction with other GCC countries have also transferred weapons to the Free Syrian Army and other armed elements that have been fighting the regime's soldiers as well as launching attacks against government targets. According to credible reports, the sophistication and quantity of these weapons funneled to the opposition by Qatar, Saudi Arabia, Jordan, and Turkey with the assistance of the United States has increased manyfold since the autumn of 2012 and especially during the early months of 2013.[7] These reports seem to be borne out by the increasing lethality of opposition attacks on regime targets. The rebel control of substantial portions of north-east Syria bordering Turkey, the partial takeover of Aleppo by insurgent groups, and their continuing encroachments into the capital Damascus are further indications that their arsenals are being adequately replenished by their foreign friends.

More recently the United States and its European allies have also decided to expand military aid to the Syrian rebel forces. What is holding back the full implementation of this decision is their fear that sophisticated weaponry may fall into the "wrong hands," by which they mean al-Qaeda-linked Islamist groups, such as the al-Nusra Front, who happen to be the best fighters among the opposition forces. However, reliable reports suggest that the tiny but gas-rich Emirate of Qatar has ignored such American and European concerns and has been supplying heat-seeking shoulder-fired missiles to rebel groups.[8] Since Qatar has a close relationship with Syrian groups linked to the Muslim Brotherhood, it is more than likely that such missiles have been provided to these groups.

All this makes clear that while foreign funding and flow of arms from abroad may not have been initially responsible for launching the anti-Assad movement in Syria, they have certainly helped in turning what started as a civilian democratic movement first into an insurgency and then into a full-fledged civil war with the attendant risk of turning the country into a failed state. This scenario will become all the more likely if the United States with or without the help of its European allies launches air attacks on Syrian military and communication facilities using the regime's employment of chemical weapons, if proven, as an excuse for such attacks. Degrading the Syrian state's capacity further could quickly turn a failing state into a failed one.

Current trends in the fighting in Syria demonstrate that the involvement of regional powers such as Saudi Arabia and Turkey on behalf of the opposition and Iran on the side of the regime has turned the conflict in Syria from a domestic to a regional affair. At the same time, it is becoming increasingly clear that what happens in and to Syria could have not merely regional but also global ramifications, thanks to the Syrian regime's strategic and economic links with Russia and the support extended to the opposition by the United States and its European allies. Russia and China have so far resisted Western calls to put pressure on Assad to resign. They have also vetoed three UN Security Council resolutions seeking to impose sanctions on

Syria. Above all, as stated earlier, Moscow is averse to a Libya-style Western intervention that would damage Russia's standing and role in Syria, its solitary ally in the Arab Mediterranean.

While the Russian connection with Syria functions as a constraint on the Western powers' proclivity to directly intervene in the country, the Assad regime's close relationship with Iran acts as an incentive for the United States to seek the regime's removal, especially in the context of the stand-off between Iran and the P5+1 (the five permanent members of the UN Security Council plus Germany) on the nuclear issue. In other words, it appears that for the Western powers a major purpose of bringing down the Assad regime is to punish Iran for its recalcitrance on the nuclear issue. Working against this logic is the fact that Western intervention to depose the Assad regime is likely to leave the United States and its allies stuck in a quagmire, since they do not seem to have a plan for post-Assad Syria or the diplomatic capabilities to back up a plan even if they had one. Washington is worried that post-Assad Syria may turn out to be a re-run of the anarchy and violence let loose by the American invasion of Iraq that has left the US image in tatters in the Middle East. A similar intervention again without the clear endorsement of the Security Council – highly unlikely because of Russian and Chinese opposition – could also embroil the Western powers, and regional allies like Turkey, in serious conflicts with Iran and Russia. This is the primary reason why the United States, while cranking up its anti-Assad rhetoric and covertly supporting the armed opposition, had until recently refrained from calling for direct military intervention to remove the Syrian regime *à la* Libya.

The use of chemical weapons in August 2013 in the Syrian civil war, it was assumed by the regime, appeared to be a game changer as far as US policy was concerned, especially because President Obama had publicly drawn a "red line" on this issue, warning Assad the previous August that the use of such weapons would lead to American retribution. It seemed at one point that American airstrikes were a distinct possibility, but, thanks to some quick-footed diplomacy by Russia and Congressional reluctance to endorse a military response, this threat has been averted for the moment.

The lack of unity among the opposition forces, including rifts between the leadership in exile and commanders of rebel forces on the ground, tensions between the Muslim Brotherhood and other political factions, and, above all, the antagonism between al-Qaeda-linked Islamist militias such as the al-Nusra Front and the more secular-minded Free Syrian Army, which has increasingly taken on the character of shooting wars, make an anarchic outcome of the Syrian problem probable, as does the fact that regional militias control what amount to fiefdoms. UN envoy to Syria Lakhdar Brahimi warned that the country might well be on its way to "Somalization," and that the lack of a negotiated agreement about a transitional government could lead to as many as 100,000 deaths in 2013.[9]

Brahimi's prediction that "[p]ouring more arms to the opposition would bring more arms to the government and that will not solve the problem"[10] has been proved correct by reports of airlift and sealift of arms to the regime by Iran and possibly Russia. As well-armed and trained opposition fighters have gained ground, it has led to the battle-hardened Lebanese Hizbullah, which considers its survival intertwined with that of the Assad regime, weighing in on behalf of the Assad government not only as trainers and military advisors but also as combatants in the civil war.

The impact of the civil war in Syria on neighboring countries, especially Lebanon and Iraq, is becoming increasingly evident. Clashes, including the bombings of both Shia and Sunni targets, have taken place among Sunni, Alawite, and Shia groups in Lebanon, threatening an already fragile polity. Iraq has not only been affected by the Syrian conflict, with by and large the Sunnis supporting the opposition and the Shia the regime, but has also exported its own sectarian and political divisions into Syria, with the Iraqi government clandestinely supporting the Assad regime and, simultaneously, al-Qaeda elements in Iraq crossing the porous border to provide some of the best fighting forces to the Sunni opponents of Assad. Some reports suggest that al-Qaeda's wing in Iraq, known as the Islamic State of Iraq, and the al-Nusra Front in Syria, which is largely funded by the former, have decided to merge into one entity called the Islamic State of Iraq and the Levant. Other reports, however, talk about rivalry as well as cooperation between the two groups and say that the al-Nusra Front has refused to merge with al-Qaeda in Iraq.

The participation of al-Qaeda-linked elements in the war against the Assad regime has created a quandary for the United States and its allies since they support the Syrian opposition, on the one hand, but loathe al-Qaeda and the Sunni militants, who form a significant portion of the armed opposition, on the other. The Shia-dominated Iraqi government's involvement in the

Syrian civil war, even if clandestinely, on Assad's side has also increased tensions between Baghdad and Washington and demonstrated that in the final analysis Iran has greater influence in Iraq than does the United States.

The Turkish conundrum

Turkey, the pivotal power in the eastern Mediterranean, also has vital interests at stake in the Syrian conflict. Not only does it share a long land border with Syria, it is the upper riparian for scarce water resources that flow into Syria, a relationship that has often created tensions between the two countries. Above all, Turkey shares the problem of Kurdish irredentism with Syria (as well as with Iraq and Iran). Turkey's relations with Syria, which had been tense during the 1980s and 1990s, began to thaw in 1998 when Damascus, which had supported the PKK against Turkey for its own reasons, expelled PKK chief Abdullah Ocalan from Syria, leading to his capture and abduction by the Turkish secret service. It improved further following the coming to power in Turkey of the AKP in 2002, especially since the appointment of Ahmet Davutoglu as Foreign Minister in 2009 and the adoption of his "zero problems with neighbors" doctrine as the basis of Turkey's foreign policy.

This policy provided positive returns for Turkey until the outbreak of the Arab Spring, which turned out to be a mixed blessing for Ankara. On the one hand, it enhanced the popularity of the Turkish model among the Arab publics, where Prime Minister Erdogan was treated like a rock star when he visited Cairo and Tunis after the overthrow of the dictators in these two countries. On the other, it posed painful choices for Ankara between its newfound, often authoritarian, friends in the Arab world and the democratic aspirations of the Arab peoples inspired in part by the success of Turkish democracy. This tension was reflected above all in Turkey's policy toward Syria once opposition to the Assad regime picked up steam. Initially the Turkish government advised Assad, who seemed to welcome such counsel, to compromise with the democracy movement and lead the way for political change in Syria. But by August 2011 Ankara concluded that Assad's promises in this regard were hypocritical and in a remarkable about-face Turkey became the principal political supporter of the anti-Assad movement as well as its primary military base, providing refuge to elements fighting the Assad regime as well as acting as the major conduit for the supply of arms to them.

Turkey's reasons for this change were manifold.

First, it concluded that its democratic credentials would be sullied if it did not support the movement for regime change in Syria, especially since it had faced harsh criticism for its silence during the Saudi-supported crackdown on the democratic movement in Bahrain. Second, it estimated that the Assad regime was doomed to fall and that Ankara must position itself as the principal benefactor of the opposition in order to reap strategic and economic benefits in the post-Assad era. Third, Turkey wanted to signal its NATO allies, especially the United States, that it was on their side in the Syrian crisis and against Iran, which had become the primary supporter of the Assad regime. Such signaling was deemed essential in order to allay Western apprehensions that Ankara had "sold out" to its Muslim neighbors, particularly Iran, at the expense of its relations with Europe and America. Fourth, Ankara seems to have been misled by the decisiveness, alacrity, and force with which NATO had responded to the Libyan crisis and expected a repetition of the same response from NATO in the case of Syria and a quick dénouement of the Assad regime. Finally, both Prime Minister Erdogan and Foreign Minister Davutoglu had invested a considerable degree of political capital in building strong relations with Assad and felt betrayed by his refusal to follow through on the promises for reform he had made to them.

As a consequence, Turkey has become deeply involved in the Syrian crisis and is in danger of being stuck in what threatens to become a quagmire. With the Syrian stalemate unlikely to be broken in the immediate future, Turkey could anticipate low-intensity warfare with the Syrian regime for a considerable period, thus draining its resources, negatively impacting its burgeoning trade with countries of the Middle East, much of which passed overland through Syria, destroying the trust it had painstakingly built in its relations with Iran, and overall upsetting its economic prospects in the long run.

If the Assad regime falls, given present indications, Turkey could be faced with an even more frightening prospect, namely, the partition of Syria into several ethnic- and sectarian-based statelets, including a Kurdish one on Turkey's borders that could further stoke Kurdish irredentism in the country despite the current thaw in the relations between the PKK and the Turkish government. Such an outcome, quite possible given the disarray among the Syrian opposition, would likely include a continuing civil war of horrific proportions among sectarian and ethnic groups, much as had happened in Afghanistan after the Soviet withdrawal and the fall of the communist regime.

There is the attendant danger that, in this event, foreign backers of the Syrian opposition, especially the United States and Saudi Arabia, would pull out precipitately and leave Syria to its fate as they did with Afghanistan in the 1990s. This scenario appears probable because these powers have their own agendas related more to weakening Iran than to democracy promotion in Syria, and their objectives would be achieved with the fall of Assad regardless of what happens to the Syrian people. Turkey, like Pakistan in the 1990s in relation to Afghanistan, will then be left to deal with the Syrian mess alone. If anarchy and terrorism come to prevail in Syria in the wake of Assad's fall, as they're likely to do given the sectarian divisions in the country and the role of militant jihadists in the war against the Assad regime, Turkey will not remain immune to the anarchy next door and could witness a marked increase in Kurdish terrorism and in the sectarian divide between Sunnis and Alevis. Although the Turkish Alevis are different from the Syrian Alawites, they empathize with the latter because of their similar nomenclature and, more importantly, because of similar fears of domination by the Sunni majority in both states.

Regional and Global Rivalries

Recent attempts by the Turkish government to negotiate a resolution of its Kurdish problem with PKK chief Abdullah Ocalan have been largely motivated by this constellation of forces and factors both within Turkey and in its immediate neighborhood that have the capacity to gravely threaten the country's security and economic prosperity in the medium term. Turkey's potential conflict of interest with Iran in Iraq, given Iran's support for the Shia-dominated al-Maliki government and Turkey's sympathy for the predominantly Sunni Iraqi opposition and its support for the autonomous Kurdish Regional Government in its disputes with Baghdad, had already muddied the waters in terms of Ankara's relations with Tehran even before the Syrian crisis erupted. Differences over Syria have strained the relationship further, even threatening a total breakdown. This may suit the interests of outside powers, especially the United States and Israel, who would like to see conflict prevail between the two most powerful Muslim states in the Middle East. However, it does not bode well for the region's future security and stability, which can only be guaranteed by a smooth working relationship between Ankara and Tehran.

As the foregoing analysis has attempted to make clear, the major reason why the current struggle for

Syria has become so immensely complicated is its very close entwinement with two related issues in which many of the same protagonists face off each other. The first of these is the struggle for influence if not control over energy-rich post-Saddam Iraq among Iran, Saudi Arabia, Turkey, and the United States. The second is the confrontation between Iran, on the one hand, and the United States, the European powers, Israel, and Saudi Arabia, on the other, on Iran's right to enrich uranium that its opponents consider a part of Tehran's design to acquire nuclear weapons capability clandestinely.

Syria has thus become a part of a region-wide tussle for supremacy or pre-eminence (call it what you like), which is essentially about the re-calibration of two inter-related balances of power: the one between Iran and Saudi Arabia in the Persian Gulf, and the other the overall balance of power in the Middle East between the American–Israeli axis and Iran. The Iranian support to Assad and the US–Saudi support to his opponents can only be understood in the context of these larger struggles for power and influence going on in the Middle East. The resolution of the Syrian crisis is therefore linked to what happens in these other arenas and cannot be addressed in isolation from them. This makes finding a solution to the

Syrian conflict enormously difficult if not totally impossible.

Bahrain

Bahrain, like Syria, is strategically very significant both globally and regionally, primarily because, as noted, it is the home of the US Fifth Fleet. Any major transformation of the domestic political order in Bahrain could threaten the naval base and thus have a major impact on American force projection capability in the Persian Gulf. This outcome would seem more than likely given the pro-Iranian sympathies of the majority Shia population in Bahrain, which would be empowered as a result of a transition to democratic rule. At a minimum a democratic Bahrain is likely to shift the psychological, if not the military, balance in Iran's favor by putting other Gulf monarchies on notice that an American military presence or security umbrella is unlikely to protect their regimes indefinitely. In fact, the fall of the Bahrain monarchy would likely convey the message that an overt American connection might be counterproductive from the perspective of regime security because of popular antipathy in the region toward the United States.

The overthrow of the Bahrain monarchy, or even a reduction in its absolute powers, would have a major impact on the regional balance between Saudi Arabia, the regime's leading protector, and Iran, whose sympathies lie with the majority of the population. It was no surprise that the Saudis, using the cover of the GCC, of which both Saudi Arabia and Bahrain are members, sent troops into Bahrain in March 2011, signaling that they were ready and willing to protect the regime at all cost. Saudi Arabia thus ensured that the hardliners within the regime, led by the Prime Minister, emerged victorious over moderates, represented by the Crown Prince, who were inclined to reach a compromise with the democracy movement. The Saudi move also emboldened the Bahraini regime to crack down sharply on the pro-democracy protestors, turning the confrontation into a zero-sum game. The Saudi interest in suppressing the Bahraini democracy movement is intimately connected to Riyadh's apprehension that its success may have a snowball effect on Saudi Arabia's own restive Shia population concentrated in the energy-rich eastern province contiguous to Bahrain.

Although it appeared initially that the regime had effectively suppressed the Bahraini opposition, this is not the case. There have been periodic eruptions of demonstrations that have been chipping away at the residual legitimacy of the ruling house. The second anniversary of the Bahraini uprising in February 2013 was marked by protests and more killings by the security forces. A rather farcical attempt at a National Dialogue that does not include government representatives was initiated by the regime but has gone nowhere. Divisions between the hardliners and moderates within the regime, within the Shia opposition, and among the Sunni minority have immensely complicated the problem. The current stalemate seems to be a precursor for another major eruption of violence, further fueling not merely sectarianism but also anti-Americanism among the population and putting at risk the future of American strategic interests in the Persian Gulf.[11]

All the examples we have analyzed in this chapter show how regional and global rivalries enormously complicate the process of transition to democratic governance in the Arab world. Transitions are always unsettling; but external involvement can turn them into serious threats to regional security and stability. Indeed several of the countries we have looked at, especially Syria and Bahrain, can easily become flashpoints triggering regional conflicts on a major scale that in turn may invite military intervention by NATO, the United States, and Russia. The vast exportable energy resources of the Middle East and its strategic location add to the possibility that any regional conflict could lead to a global confrontation, thus negatively impacting the security and stability of the international system as a whole. And that's before we have considered the mounting international tensions caused by Iran's nuclear ambitions, to which we will turn in the next chapter.

5

Iran and "the Bomb"

During the past few years the issue of the Iranian "bomb" has overshadowed most other concerns in the West relating to the Middle East, including the Israel–Palestine conflict. Stopping Iran from achieving presumed nuclear weapons capability has become the top foreign policy priority not only for Israel and the United States but also for all major Western powers and has come to dominate the UN Security Council agenda as well. Unprecedentedly stringent economic sanctions have been imposed on Iran by the Security Council at the behest of the United States and its allies. Additionally, the United States and the EU have unilaterally imposed further sanctions that go beyond those imposed by the Security Council to economically strangle Iran, thus forcing it to give up its drive to enrich uranium domestically.

However, the sanctions have had a mixed, some would argue counterproductive, effect. In the words of one well-informed former Iranian policy-maker, who worked for years in high positions related to nuclear diplomacy, "Simply put, if the real objective of the sanctions was to hurt ordinary Iranians, they have been successful. If they were intended to compel Iran to cease its current nuclear program, they have not only failed, but have actually resulted in acceleration of the program." He goes on to point out that,

> As reports by the International Atomic Energy Agency indicate, prior to sanctions related to its nuclear program, Iran had one uranium enrichment site, a pilot plant of 164 centrifuges enriching uranium at a level of 3.5%, one generation of centrifuges and an approximately 100 kg stockpile of enriched uranium. Today, it has two enrichment sites with roughly 12,000 centrifuges, can enrich uranium up to 20%, possesses a new generation of centrifuges and has amassed a stockpile of more than 8,000 kg of enriched uranium.[1]

It is estimated that out of this stockpile, 123 kilograms consists of uranium enriched up to 20 percent.[2]

The intense pressure that the Western members of the P5+1 have put on Tehran to forgo its right to enrich uranium guaranteed by the Nuclear Non-Proliferation Treaty (NPT) further points to the importance accorded to this subject by some of the most powerful members of the international community. Iran has been partially responsible for the tough stand taken by the United States and the EU countries by engaging clandestinely in activities such as building a hardened nuclear enrichment plant in Natanz, a heavy water research reactor at Arak, and an underground uranium enrichment facility in Fordow near the holy city of Qom. Tehran did not disclose these activities to the International Atomic Energy Agency (IAEA) until forced to do so after information about the first two surfaced in 2002 and about the third in 2009, largely through the work of Israeli and American intelligence agencies. Furthermore, Tehran clandestinely bought centrifuges and centrifuge technology from the network of the Pakistani rogue nuclear scientist A.Q. Khan. This fact also came to light several years after the centrifuges had been installed in Iran.

Such covert activities led the IAEA to refer the matter to the Security Council in 2006, which decided to impose economic sanctions on Iran the following year. These sanctions were further toughened by subsequent resolutions passed in 2008 and 2010 at the insistence of the Western powers in order to stifle the Iranian economy and force Tehran to end its uranium enrichment program. Efforts in 2010 by then Security Council members Turkey and Brazil to break the impasse by persuading Iran to ship most of its enriched uranium abroad came to naught after Iran had indicated its acceptance of the plan because of America's opposition to a potential agreement that initially seemed to have Washington's blessing.

Apprehension in the West that Iran is clandestinely engaged in building nuclear weapons lies at the heart of the debate – to bomb Iran or live with the Iranian bomb – surrounding the country's nuclear program, which Tehran insists is solely for civilian purposes. The debate continues despite the fact that the authoritative US National Intelligence Estimate (NIE) in a report in 2007 concluded that Iran stopped work on a nuclear weapons program in 2003. According to the *New York Times*, the 2010 version of the NIE assessment on Iran, although not made public, "concluded that while Iran had conducted some basic weapons-related research, it was not believed to have restarted the actual weapons program halted in 2003."[3]

A recent assessment provided by the US Director of National Intelligence to the House Select Committee on Intelligence on April 11, 2013, seemed to be deliberately worded so vaguely as to cover all contingencies. It read in part:

> We assess Iran is developing nuclear capabilities to enhance its security, prestige, and regional influence and give it the ability to develop nuclear weapons, should a decision be made to do so. We do not know if Iran will eventually decide to build nuclear weapons. Tehran has developed technical expertise in a number of areas – including uranium enrichment, nuclear reactors, and ballistic missiles – from which it could draw if it decided to build missile-deliverable nuclear weapons. These technical advancements strengthen our assessment that Iran has the scientific, technical, and industrial capacity to eventually produce nuclear weapons. This makes the central issue its political will to do so. Of particular note, Iran has made progress during the past year that better positions it to produce weapons-grade uranium (WGU) using its declared facilities and uranium stockpiles, should it choose to do so. *Despite this progress, we assess Iran could not divert safeguarded material and produce a weapon-worth of WGU before this activity is discovered.*[4]

Despite the generally vague and hesitant character of estimates at the highest levels of the US intelligence community, the speculation about Iran's imminent nuclear capability goes on (although the

117

target is moved back yearly). Explicit threats by Israel and implied ones by the United States about launching attacks on Iranian nuclear facilities – with the constant reiteration by senior American officials, including the President, that "all options are on the table" – continue to proliferate. We therefore need to dig further into the real reasons behind this brouhaha. These reasons cannot be fully understood unless one analyzes the controversy surrounding Iran's nuclear aspiration in relation to two very important variables that affect the country's decision-making on the nuclear issue as well as impact the perceptions of all parties involved in this debate.

The Israeli nuclear arsenal

The first of these variables is Israel's possession of a formidable nuclear arsenal and sophisticated delivery systems to match that make it the sole nuclear weapons power in the Middle East. More important, Israel has consistently implied in terms of its rhetoric and policy that, given its security situation, it must monopolize nuclear weapons capability in the Middle East since a regional balance that is based on nuclear deterrence will, in

Israeli perceptions, have highly negative effects on its freedom of action in the region. It is this consideration, more than anything else, which drives Israeli opposition to the Iranian nuclear enrichment program since it has the potential to provide Iran with a credible nuclear weapons option and even a second-strike capability at some stage in the future that could change the overall balance of forces in the Middle East.

Although Israel does not officially acknowledge that it is in possession of nuclear weapons capability, it has been known to Western intelligence communities at least since the late 1960s and became public knowledge in the early 1970s. The Israeli nuclear arsenal has now grown to several hundred nuclear warheads of different sizes and sophistication as well as highly sophisticated delivery systems, including missiles that can reach Iran.[5] A clear indication of Israel's desire to preserve its nuclear weapons option was its refusal to sign the NPT, which was opened for signature in 1968 and came into force in 1970. Israel suffered no negative consequences from remaining outside the NPT regime in terms of its relations with the United States, which had been putting great pressure on other "threshold" countries, such as Brazil and India, to sign and ratify the treaty or face penalties in terms of access to nuclear technology for peaceful purposes. Israel continues to resist calls to make its nuclear program transparent and bring it within the ambit of the NPT.

Incidentally, Iran was one of the first countries to sign and ratify the NPT. Although there were indications that the Shah, who then held absolute power in Iran, was interested in acquiring nuclear weapons at some stage, his primary interest was to keep on the right side of the United States for strategic and economic reasons as well as considerations of regime security. Signing the NPT in combination with Tehran's strategic alliance with the United States assured Iran unfettered access to nuclear material and knowhow from the West essential for the civilian nuclear program for energy generation in which the Shah had invested massively. This goal would have suffered great harm had Iran not signed the NPT. It is instructive to note, however, that the father of the Iranian nuclear program, Akbar Etemad, who was a close confidant of the Shah, was opposed to Iran signing the NPT because "he believed [it] threatened Iran's national sovereignty,"[6] implying that Iran would be giving up its nuclear weapons option for ever. However, the Shah overruled him on this issue, the only occasion, according to Etemad, when the

Shah did not accept his advice relating to nuclear matters.

Given Israel's nuclear capability and its conventional military might demonstrated in several wars against Arab adversaries, it poses, in the eyes of the Iranian policy-makers, a credible military, including nuclear, threat to their country, especially since relations between Israel and Iran have been hostile for most of the period following the Iranian Revolution of 1979. This has been the case because of Israel's refusal to withdraw from the Palestinian territories occupied in 1967 and the Islamic Republic's commitment to the Palestinian cause and to the liberation of Islam's holy sites in Jerusalem from Israeli control.

The Iranians perceive it as a grave injustice that the major powers have taken little note of Israel's nuclear weapons stockpile thanks to its special relationship with the United States, while putting pressure on Iran to give up its right to nuclear enrichment. Israel's potential nuclear threat plus the refusal of the major powers to put pressure on it to make its nuclear program transparent and subject it to IAEA inspections by signing the NPT provide Iran with part of the rationale for building nuclear weapons, if it decides to do so, in order to deter and balance Israel's nuclear capability.

Iran and "the Bomb"

The United States and Iran

The second, and probably more important, motive for Iran's search for nuclear capability is the hostile relationship between the United States and the Islamic Republic of Iran from the time of the Iranian Revolution in 1979. Many analysts consider the revolution to be at least in part a delayed reaction to the American-engineered coup in 1953 that overthrew Iran's democratically elected government and restored the Shah to the throne. The revolution was followed several months later by a group of Iranian students taking American diplomats hostage, with the post-facto blessing of Ayatollah Khomeini, and holding them for 444 days. Their justification was that they were paying America back in its own coin since, according to them, the United States had held the entire Iranian nation "hostage" between 1953 and 1979 by putting the Shah back on the throne and supporting absolute rule by a monarch who essentially did Washington's bidding. The hostage crisis led to a total rupture in relations between the United States and Iran, a situation that has continued until today.

These two seminal events of 1953 and 1979 that demonstrate the unremitting mutual hostility between Iran and the United States largely determine the lenses through which Washington and Tehran view each other. This is very clear in the case of Iran's nuclear program and the vastly different perceptions that the United States and Iran exhibit on this issue. Most analysts make the mistake of confusing cause with effect in their treatment of Iran's nuclear policy and Iranian–American relations. Iranian nuclear aspirations are not the cause of hostile relations with the United States. Rather, hostile relations with the United States have led Tehran to increasingly commit itself to safeguard its nuclear weapons option. The problem is, therefore, intensely political and psychological and cannot be reduced to the technical issue of whether Iran is or is not in compliance with certain of its obligations as a non-nuclear signatory to the NPT.

In fact, the NPT never seemed to be a major issue for Iran – the Shah signed it in 1968, abjuring Iran's right to develop nuclear weapons capability despite the fact that, according to Akbar Etemad, "the Shah wanted to leave all options on the table in terms of developing a nuclear bomb."[7] In the same vein, after the Islamic Revolution of 1979, Iran's Supreme Leader Ayatollah Khomeini declared weapons of mass destruction (WMDs) to be un-Islamic because they violated the Islamic injunction that innocent people must not be harmed during a war. It was the eight-year-long Iran–Iraq War (1980–8), during which Iraq used chemical weapons and was, as the Osirak reactor and the Israeli attack on it in 1981 demonstrated, in obvious pursuit of nuclear weapons that led to the change of heart regarding nuclear weapons and their efficacy among the Iranian political elite. This motivated Iran to revive its civilian nuclear program, especially the Bushehr nuclear power plant, which had been in limbo since the revolution and had also been seriously damaged by Iraqi airstrikes. Tehran's renewed interest in nuclear energy could also be interpreted as the first step toward eventually acquiring the knowledge of how to operate the full nuclear cycle, thus moving closer to achieving weapons capability.

When the Iran–Iraq War came to an end in 1988, Iraq was replaced by the United States in Iranian perceptions as the major strategic threat to the country. The very explicit anti-Iranian stance adopted by Washington during the last phase of that war, which included among other things the shooting down of an Iranian civilian airliner in 1988, convinced the Iranian regime of America's malevolent intentions toward it. Iranian apprehensions were augmented by the massive deployment of US troops and weaponry in and around the Persian Gulf region as a build-up to the First Gulf

War of 1991 and its continued overt military presence in the area following its success in evicting Iraq from Kuwait. These actions convinced the Iranian elite that the United States intended to politically and militarily dominate the energy-rich region and that such domination would have deleterious consequences for Iranian interests and aspirations.

It was clear that the American strategy toward the Persian Gulf had changed beginning with the Operations Desert Shield (1990) and Desert Storm (1991). Washington had given up on regional surrogates defending its interests in the region while it positioned its reserve naval power offshore. It was now committed to massively deploying troops on the ground, thus signaling clearly that it was the unrivaled and unmediated military hegemon in and around the Persian Gulf. Iran had, therefore, to re-evaluate its own strategy in response to this fundamental change in American policy in order to meet a qualitatively different challenge from the United States compared to the indirect threat it had faced so far. Nuclear weapons presumably became a part of Tehran's new calculus of deterrence against the overwhelming might of the lone superpower, whose military might was now directly deployed in Iran's vicinity.

Iran's apprehension of American intentions and

of American military power was greatly exacerbated by the "war on terror" launched by the
United States in the first decade of this century. This
led to the American and allied military invasion of
two countries contiguous to Iran: Afghanistan and
Iraq. The invasions led to an almost decade-long
American occupation of Iraq, the installation of an
American-sponsored government in Afghanistan,
and the continuing presence of American and allied
NATO troops in that country expected to last
at least until the end of 2014. Iranian fears of
encirclement increased further with the establishment of American military bases in neighboring
Uzbekistan and Tajikistan to support the war effort
in Afghanistan against al-Qaeda and the Taliban
and, when they were defeated, to act as the rear
bases for troops deployed in Afghanistan to fight
the renewed Taliban-led insurgency. This American
military presence on the ground in Iran's vicinity,
when combined with the American armada, con-
sisting of both conventional and nuclear weapons,
assembled in the Persian Gulf and the Arabian Sea,
convinced the Iranian leadership that Washington
had Tehran in its cross-hairs and was likely to
turn its attention toward Iran once it has completed the conquest of Iraq and the pacification of
Afghanistan.

Iran and "the Bomb"

The straw that broke the Iranian camel's back was President George W. Bush's characterization of Iran in his State of the Union address in January 2002 as a member of the "axis of evil" together with Iraq and North Korea. Although some of the Iranian clandestine activity preceded this statement, its impact on Iranian policy-makers was heightened by the fact that it came within weeks of the Bonn conference on Afghanistan in December 2001. Iran had cooperated with the United States at that conference to anoint the American-chosen Hamid Karzai as the President of post-Taliban Afghanistan. Had Iran decided not to do so, it had sufficient clout among Afghanistan's Tajik-dominated Northern Alliance, the Shia Hazaras of central Afghanistan, and Tajik warlord Ismail Khan, who controlled Herat in western Afghanistan, to abort America's bid to appoint Karzai President. James Dobbins, the chief American representative at the Bonn meeting, testified to the astonishing amount of cooperation he received at that conference from Iranian Deputy Foreign Minister Javad Zarif, who went out of his way to convince Iran's allies in Afghanistan to cooperate with the American plan. In his testimony before the House Subcommittee on National Security and Foreign Affairs of the US Congress on November 7, 2007, Dobbins stated categorically that "Zarif had achieved the final breakthrough without which the Karzai government might never have been formed."[8]

In this context of Iran's demonstration of goodwill toward the United States over Afghanistan, the "axis of evil" statement not only shocked the Iranian leadership, it convinced it that the United States' primary goal regarding Iran was forcibly to bring about regime change just as it had done in Iraq. Tehran was further convinced that the United States aimed in the guise of bringing about regime change to debilitate Iran's military capability, as it had done with Iraq, to the point where it would no longer be able to act as a potential deterrent to Israel's hegemonial aspirations in the Middle East.

It would not be wrong to assume, therefore, that Washington's hostility toward the Iranian regime coupled with the United States' massive conventional and nuclear capability deployed on land and sea around Iran provided Tehran with the necessary justification for accelerating the development of nuclear weapons capability as a deterrent against American military intervention in the country à la Iraq. One can assume that this option appeared particularly attractive to Tehran in light of the differential treatment meted out by the United States to nuclear-armed North Korea as compared to non-nuclear Iraq and later to Qaddafi's Libya after it had voluntarily abandoned its very rudimentary nuclear weapons program in order to appease Western concerns.

In addition to Tehran's security concerns regarding Israel and the United States, one should note that Iran has several nuclear-armed neighbors – Russia, China, Pakistan, and India – in its vicinity. Such a strategic landscape detracts from Iran's effort to be recognized as a major regional player as long as it remains without nuclear weapons capability or at least the material and the knowhow to produce nuclear weapons at relatively short notice. This was recognized by none other than Israel's former hardline Defense Minister Ehud Barak, who had stridently argued for the United States and Israel to attack Iran in order to denude it of its nuclear capabilities. In a candid moment, Barak recognized the strategic rationality of Iran's pursuit of nuclear weapons capability. In an appearance in November 2011 on the highly regarded PBS show *Charlie Rose*, he was asked whether he would want to acquire nuclear weapons if he were an Iranian government minister. Barak responded very unequivocally: "Probably, probably. I know it's not – I mean I don't delude myself that they are doing it just because of Israel. They look around, they see the Indians are nuclear, the Chinese are nuclear, Pakistan is nuclear, not to mention the Russians."[9] It is clear that Iran exists in a neighborhood where nuclear weapons are viewed as a currency both of power and of prestige and this makes it harder for Tehran to renounce the nuclear weapons option for good, something that even the pro-American Shah had not contemplated.

Unresolved issues

The desire to acquire nuclear weapons for purposes of either deterrence or prestige or both is very different from using such weapons for aggressive purposes. It is this leap from the former assumption to the latter on the part of Western analysts and policy-makers that has enormously complicated negotiations between the P5+1 and Iran on the latter's nuclear enrichment program. It has done so because it does not give adequate weight to Iran's security and prestige concerns and is not interested in addressing these facets of the issue. No solution acceptable to Tehran can be found unless these very important motivations for Iran's nuclear program are addressed.

The alternative to this route is likely to end in

a major catastrophe such as an invasion of Iran, which can be expected to have unpredictable consequences. This latter option continues to be on the cards, especially since the Israeli Prime Minister Benjamin Netanyahu is pushing for it and the ongoing negotiations between the P5+1 and Iran have not closed the wide gap between the two sides' positions on Iran's right to enrich uranium. EU foreign policy chief Catherine Ashton clearly reflected this sentiment when she announced at the end of the round of talks in Almaty, Kazakhstan, in April 2013 that the two sides remained far apart concerning the substantial issues.

When one cuts through all the jargon surrounding these negotiations, it becomes clear that there are several points that remain irreconcilable within the present framework. The first is Iran's insistence that the P5+1 unconditionally recognize Iran's right to enrich uranium to levels required for civilian purposes, a right it argues is guaranteed by Article 4 of the NPT. The P5+1 have consistently refused to accept this right, despite the fact that it is enshrined in the NPT. While some of this reluctance may be attributed to Iran's efforts to hide part of its nuclear program from IAEA inspectors, it now seems to have become a matter of principle for the Western powers, transcending acts of omission and commission by Tehran. The second is Iran's insistence that any concession it makes on the issue of nuclear enrichment must be immediately matched by the lifting of major economic sanctions imposed upon it by the UN Security Council and unilaterally by the United States and the EU and that the P5+1 immediately and explicitly put this quid pro quo on the table rather than making vague statements that the lifting of sanctions incrementally depends upon Iran's "behavior."

The P5+1 insist, however, that Iran must not enrich uranium domestically and that fuel rods must be shipped out for enrichment and returned to Iran for civilian purposes under IAEA or other international supervision. The basic idea here is not merely to monitor to what degree Iranian uranium is enriched but also to dismantle existing Iranian uranium enrichment facilities, thus denying Iran the option of improving upon its enrichment capabilities, which, it is presumed, Tehran will use for manufacturing weapons-grade material. Iran finds this demand not only onerous but also a derogation of its sovereignty.

Furthermore, the P5+1 (especially its four Western members) are reluctant to lift major sanctions in return for Iranian commitments not to enrich uranium beyond a certain level, probably

20 percent, well below the threshold required for manufacturing weapons. The P5+1 insist that they will lift such sanctions only piece-meal, with the most inconsequential ones first depending upon Iran's actions aimed at relinquishing its uranium enrichment capability. The major sanctions, the P5+1 argue, will be rescinded only at the end of this process if the P5+1 are satisfied that Iran is totally in compliance with their demands. Tehran finds this unacceptable because, in the words of a well-informed Iranian analyst, "the P5+1 ... ask Iran to give diamonds in return for peanuts. ... Asking Iran to stop twenty percent [uranium enrichment] ... [and] to give access to the IAEA beyond [the] Additional Protocol – this is practically the diamonds the P5+1 want. ... If they are going to propose Iran spare parts for airplanes [in exchange], these would be peanuts."[10]

Several times in the past few years it appeared as if Israel and the United States were moving inexorably toward a military showdown with Iran, beginning with airstrikes on Iran's nuclear facilities to retard the progress of the Iranian nuclear program by several years. Such an exercise, actively propagated by the Israelis, would likely spin out of control and involve the United States in a major confrontation with Iran, which has vowed to retaliate by attacking not only American and Israeli targets but also those of America's regional allies, such as Saudi Arabia, Bahrain, and Qatar, that house very important American military bases that are likely to be used against the country.

Furthermore, Iran has sufficient clout with important groups in Iraq and Afghanistan to make life extremely difficult for the United States and its allies in both countries. It is unlikely that an attack on Iran will not negatively affect America's relations with the Shia-dominated Iraqi government, which has until now tried to carefully balance its relations with the two adversaries with the understanding and cooperation of Iran. Iran's capacity to create mayhem in Afghanistan should not be underrated. Any attack on Iran is bound to unleash unprecedented acts of terror against American and allied troops stationed in Afghanistan and against the American-backed government in Kabul. Iran's Lebanese ally, Hizbullah, is certain to attack Israeli targets with missiles in the event of an attack on Iran, thus opening another front in the war.

Iran has also declared that it will block the Straits of Hormuz to shipping if it is attacked, thus choking off the flow of crude – about one-fifth of the world's oil flows through these Straits – from the Persian Gulf producers to the international market. Regardless of its success in the long run in being able to do so, the fear of this happening would drive tanker insurance rates and oil prices through the roof, thus hurting the currently delicately poised global economy. America's reputation in the Muslim world, already at a historic low, would nosedive further, despite the private applause it might receive from the House of Saud and some of the Gulf monarchies. Notwithstanding the Sunni–Shia rift in the Middle East, an American and/or Israeli attack on Iranian nuclear facilities would augment the conclusion already held by a significant segment of Muslim opinion, both Sunni and Shia, that the United States is engaged in a war against Islam. Terrorist sleeper cells in the United States and more particularly in Europe would in all probability be activated and would attempt to create pandemonium in the industrialized West. Even if only a part of this scenario were to unfold, it would severely and probably irrevocably damage American strategic and economic interests in the Middle East.

Additionally, the general consensus within the American strategic community, as reflected in a report written by highly respected national security analysts and former policy-makers in the United States for the Iran Project, suggests that extended military strikes by the U.S. alone or in concert with Israel could destroy or severely damage the six most important known nuclear facilities in Iran, setting back Iran's nuclear program for up to four years. Our informed estimate is that a military strike by Israel alone could delay Iran's ability to build a bomb for up to two years.[11]

It is clear that at the end of this highly risky adventure, the Iranian nuclear program would be set back only by a few years and, more importantly, Iran would re-double its efforts to acquire nuclear weapons capability and would do so openly after leaving the NPT. It would also give an additional lease of life to the current regime, solidify public opinion behind it, and turn the only pro-Western populace in the Middle East firmly against the United States and Europe. Such an exercise might temporarily extend Israel's nuclear monopoly in the Middle East but at tremendous cost to American and European interests in the region.

The way out

The only way out of this conundrum for the United States and the West is to actively and genuinely support the setting up of a Middle East

Nuclear Weapons-Free Zone (MENWFZ) that would include both Israel and Iran. Conventional wisdom in the United States and much of Europe normally rules out such an option because of the Israeli political establishment's opposition to it. It is assumed that this would automatically translate into Washington considering it a non-starter because of AIPAC's clout with the legislative and executive branches of government in the United States. However, such pessimism regarding Israeli attitudes on the MENWFZ issue is contradicted by a 2012 poll which showed that 64 percent of Israeli Jews "favored the idea of a nuclear-free zone, even when it was explained that this would mean Israel giving up its nuclear weapons . . . [and] sixty percent of respondents favored 'a system of full international inspections' of all nuclear facilities, including Israel's and Iran's, as a step toward regional disarmament."[12]

The MENWFZ has been on the table for a long time, at least since a UN General Assembly resolution, sponsored by Egypt and Iran, seeking the establishment of such a zone was passed in 1974. It is routinely brought up by Middle Eastern signatories of the NPT at its five-year review conferences. Iran has supported calls for a MENWFZ for several years, most recently at a Nuclear Disarmament

Conference it hosted in April 2010, as long as it included Israel as well as Iran. The final document of the May 2010 NPT Review conference called for the convening in 2012 of a conference of all Middle Eastern states to move forward on a 1995 proposal for a nuclear-free Middle East. It also called on Israel to sign the NPT and place "all its nuclear facilities under comprehensive IAEA ... safeguards." Israel promptly rejected the call.

Iran had initially made its participation in the MENWFZ conference conditional on Israel signing the NPT but reversed this decision in a surprise move in November 2012. However, the conference which was to be held in Helsinki, Finland, in mid-December 2012 was postponed until some time in 2013, primarily because of Israel's reluctance to participate in it under the auspices of the NPT. The conference was eventually scuttled by the United States, which issued a statement on November 23, 2012, declaring in what seemed to be a cover for the Israeli position that "the conference cannot be convened because of present conditions in the Middle East and the fact that states in the region have not reached agreement on acceptable conditions for a conference."[13]

Despite this setback, envisioning a MENWFZ is not a utopian exercise. The only alternative to the

Iran and "the Bomb"

Middle East being declared a nuclear weapons-free zone is a prolonged period of instability marked by Israeli and American threats of war against Iran or an actual invasion that could lead to uncertain, dangerous, and counterproductive outcomes. As projected earlier, an invasion of Iran is unlikely to stop the Iranian weapons program; it is only likely to accelerate it. This could lead to repeated Israeli and American strikes against Iranian nuclear facilities every couple of years, with disastrous consequences both for American interests in the Middle East and for the stability of the region. Alternatively, a condition of unstable deterrence between Israel and Iran would persist for several years or even decades until both develop second-strike capabilities and stabilize the state of deterrence on the basis of Mutual Assured Destruction (MAD). At the same time, other states in the region, such as Turkey and Saudi Arabia, may feel compelled to launch covert and unacknowledged weapons programs of their own that could set off a proliferation chain in the Middle East. The MENWFZ thus appears to be the least unsafe option in this context if the United States can be persuaded to support the establishment of such a zone as well as put pressure on Israel to come on board by giving it iron-clad security guarantees and bringing it under the American nuclear security umbrella. In any case, such a security umbrella is the de facto reality; all Washington has to do is to turn it into a de jure one.

The other major hurdle to successfully managing the Iranian nuclear issue is the lack of trust between the United States and Iran that has persisted since the Iranian Revolution of 1979. Political and psychological barriers on both sides will have to be overcome to re-build mutual trust. However, this can only be done if Washington and Tehran learn from the lessons of the past, especially of missed opportunities, and refrain from threatening one another to placate allies or domestic constituencies.[14]

The election of the moderate cleric Hassan Rouhani to the Iranian Presidency in June 2013 and his inauguration in August 2013 have opened up a new opportunity for the United States to engage with Iran on the whole gamut of issues that divide the two countries. Rouhani was Iran's chief nuclear negotiator between 2003 and 2005 when Tehran temporarily suspended its nuclear enrichment activities as a confidence-building measure in the context of discussions on the issue with major European powers. Rouhani faced a great deal of criticism within Iran for what was interpreted by large segments of the Iranian political elite as a major concession, especially since it did not lead to an adequately positive response from the Western powers. The decision was reversed when Mahmoud Ahmadinejad was elected President in 2005.

Notwithstanding this experience, Rouhani is known to be better disposed to the idea of a deal with the P5+1, and especially with the United States, on the nuclear issue than his predecessor. The fact that he has appointed Javad Zarif as his Foreign Minister is an indication of his willingness to show greater flexibility in dealing with America: Zarif was one of the principal members of Rouhani's team during the negotiations leading to the Iranian decision in 2003 to suspend uranium enrichment. As stated above, Zarif was also the principal Iranian architect of the agreement at Bonn in 2002 that led to the installation of America's favorite, Hamid Karzai, as President of Afghanistan. Zarif, who received his doctorate from the University of Denver and is a fluent English-speaker, is viewed both within and outside Iran as a voice of reason and moderation when it comes to relations with the United States. This is one of the reasons why he was sidelined during Ahmadinejad's presidency. Zarif is also tipped to be appointed the lead nuclear negotiator for the next round of talks with the P5+1. It is estimated that the Rouhani–Zarif team will in all probability be willing to introduce greater transparency regarding the Iranian nuclear program and may even permit the IAEA access to the Parchin military site near Tehran, which it has been demanding, under certain conditions.

However, the change of guard in Tehran is unlikely by itself to solve the fundamental issues causing tensions between Iran and the United States. These issues cannot be resolved until and unless a comprehensive strategic dialogue is instituted between the two governments. A strategy aimed only at addressing the controversy surrounding Iran's nuclear enrichment program, or using it as a stick to beat Iran with, in isolation from other issues and concerns bedeviling the American–Iranian relationship will be doomed to failure even under a Rouhani presidency. This will be the case because decision-makers' personal preferences and even the character of regimes cannot trump national interests, which transcend personality traits and regime attributes. It is deep-seated national interest concerns that drive Iran's policy toward the United States, and therefore they need to be addressed with sensitivity and understanding in order to bring back a degree of civility in Iranian–American relations.

It is important, therefore, that Washington

seriously consider taking the opportunity presented by a new and more reasonable President in Iran to begin a bilateral dialogue that goes well beyond the nuclear enrichment issue and deals, among other matters, with Iran's role as a pivotal power in the Persian Gulf and its aspiration to be recognized as a major actor within the broader Middle Eastern region. What is needed is an American–Iranian strategic dialogue, which will inevitably run into many rounds, to discuss how these Iranian objectives can be reconciled with American security and economic interests in the region. An American–Iranian rapprochement cannot be achieved without recognition of the fact that the dispute over Iran's nuclear enrichment program is merely a symptom of the fundamental malaise affecting these relations and not its root cause. If, however, this fact is not acknowledged and military action is undertaken against Iran, either in concert by the United States and Israel or by Israel alone, it is likely to engulf the Middle East in a confrontation before which the "war on terror" and the American invasions of Afghanistan and Iraq will pale into insignificance.

6

Will the Middle East Implode?

The Arab Spring is running out of steam, leaving in its wake a slew of broken political systems, failing states, proxy wars, and increased prospects for the re-emergence of Islamist radicalism. This was not the future of the Arab world that many analysts had imagined in the initial heady months of the Arab uprisings that had impacted almost all parts of the Middle East from North Africa to the Persian Gulf.

It is clear that the impact of these uprisings upon state structures in the Arab world has often been unsettling. As earlier chapters have explained, fragile states such as Libya, Syria, and Yemen, where the concept of state and nation do not clearly coincide and where authoritarian regimes were the principal glue holding the state together, have experienced state disintegration in varying degrees. In Libya and Yemen the writ of the central government often did not extend beyond the capital and major provincial cities, and the ruthless personality of the dictator and tribal ties substituted for the bond of citizenship provided by cohesive societies and legitimate political institutions. It was but a short step for them to lurch toward near-total state failure.

Yemen is in a state of disarray, threatened by revolt in the north and secession in the south with its political elite unable to reconcile fundamental geographic, ideological, tribal, and personal differences. Libya is a torn society as well in both geographic and tribal terms. Furthermore, the Libyan state's reach is highly circumscribed with dozens of militias taking the law into their hands. These autonomous actors with weapons have been increasingly exporting Libya's problems and conflicts to its southern neighbors, especially Mali. It is becoming clear that the primary factor that has saved Libya and Yemen from total dissolution is their recognition as juridical entities by other members of the international system.

Syria, which had exuded the image of a strong state, was shown up as a colossus with feet of clay. The Assad regime's brutal repression over the past four decades not only hid the underlying fragility of state institutions but also helped to delegitimize not merely the regime but the state as well. Bashar al-Assad's decision to fight the insurgency to the finish and the motley character of the opposition now threaten the very existence of the Syrian state as a single, united entity. The division of the Syrian state on sectarian and ethnic lines appears a distinct possibility following the fall of the Assad regime, if it takes place.

The reported use of chemical weapons in August 2013 in the Syrian civil war, generally attributed to the regime's forces, has added further complexity to the Syrian conflict. This is the case because President Obama had in August 2012 asserted that the use of chemical weapons in the Syrian conflict is a "red line" and that the United States will respond with force if this line is crossed by the Syrian regime.

Egypt's military coup

But even in Egypt, where national identity largely converges with that of the state and the integrity of the state is not in question, the uprising has exacerbated social cleavages and ideological divisions that threaten to rip apart the societal fabric. It is true that democratic transitions are nonlinear; normally they face many roadblocks on the way and suffer from periodic setbacks. Yet the Arab Spring has experienced its most dramatic and possibly irreversible setback in this most important Arab country. The removal of Egypt's first elected government in July 2013 by a military coup d'état, the incarceration and persecution of the erstwhile ruling party's leadership by the military, and the indiscriminate massacre of pro-Brotherhood demonstrators by the army and the police, leading to more than a thousand deaths, are in essence a throwback to the darkest days of the Mubarak dictatorship, despite the approval that some of these actions have received from cheering crowds in Tahrir Square. But as one commentator has pointed out,

> This time, the military agreed with the protesters. But next time, when protesters call for something that isn't in the army's interest, they will meet a very different fate. Today they are called "the people"; tomorrow they will be labeled seditious saboteurs. A year from now, the dreamy youth who celebrated and danced when Mr. Morsi was overthrown may well find themselves in the cell next door to the Brotherhood.[1]

It is true that President Morsi and the Muslim Brotherhood committed major mistakes, including railroading a constitution through the Constituent Assembly in the absence of opposition members.

One should note, however, that the constitution was put to a referendum and approved by nearly two-thirds of the voters. Furthermore, many of the Muslim Brotherhood's "excesses" were forced upon it by the uncooperative, indeed downright obstructionist, strategies employed by the secular opposition parties. Among other things, this made the Brotherhood all the more dependent on the salafi parties to its right with their more extremist Islamist agendas, some of which were reflected in the constitution drafted under Morsi's watch.

Moreover, the judiciary, especially the Constitutional Court, whose members were Mubarak-era appointees and continued to be loyal to the old regime, did its utmost to prevent the functioning of parliamentary institutions and the establishment of constitutional government. Morsi's inability to control the police, again staffed by holdovers from the Mubarak era who engaged in deliberately fostering chaos, contributed to the sense of executive indecisiveness and added to the insecurity experienced by the Egyptian people during the one year of the Brotherhood's rule. Above all, Morsi's decision to permit the military to retain its corporate, including budgetary, autonomy shielded it from civilian oversight and public accountability. This combined with the fact that he appointed the military chief, General Sisi, who he mistakenly believed was an ideological comrade, as Defense Minister meant that the President, although nominally the Supreme Commander of the Armed Forces, completely lost control of the primary coercive apparatus of the state, thus paving the way for the coup d'état that removed him from office in July 2013.

The overthrow of Egypt's first elected President and government does not bode well for the future of democracy either in Egypt or in the wider Arab world. Given Egypt's traditional leadership role in the Arab world, the Egyptian uprising, even more than its Tunisian counterpart, which preceded it by a few weeks, had heralded the beginning of the Arab Spring. Similarly, the forced removal of the elected government that the Egyptian Spring produced is likely to herald the end of that heady era. It could well be the last nail in the coffin of the Arab Spring, already teetering on the edge of the grave with a bloody civil war raging in Syria, brutal suppression of democracy activists in Bahrain, and near-chaos in Libya and Yemen. One wonders how long Tunisia, which is also ruled by an Islamist party faced with street protests, will be able to hold out as a bastion of democracy in this unfriendly environment.

Will the Middle East Implode?

Boost to Islamist radicalism

The overthrow of the Muslim Brotherhood-led government in Egypt, the cradle of political Islam in the Arab world, is also expected to seriously erode the credibility of moderate, constitutionalist Islamists across the region. As pointed out in chapter 2, the Egyptian Brotherhood had undergone a remarkable transformation beginning in the 1970s. It had shed its militant past and decided to play the political game within constitutional constraints even when, as until 2011, the constitutional cards were stacked against it. In other words, its political pragmatism had trumped ideological purity and led to its internalization of the values of compromise and the political give and take that lies at the heart of democracy. Morsi's election was the crowning act in this drama, signifying that the Islamist mainstream saw no contradiction in working within a democratic system and accepting the rules of the game without shedding its Islamist orientation.

The electoral performance of the Egyptian Brotherhood was a major victory for moderate Islamists in the intra-Islamist battle on the issue of whether democracy is compatible with Islam and, more importantly, whether Islamist parties, if they come to power, will be allowed to govern without hindrance by domestic and external forces opposed to them. The major lesson that Islamists in the Middle East are likely to learn from President Morsi's overthrow and the brutal suppression that has followed is that they will not be allowed to exercise power no matter how many compromises they make, as the Egyptian Brotherhood had done, in both the domestic and foreign policy arenas. This is likely to push a substantial portion of mainstream Islamists into the arms of the extremists who reject democracy and ideological compromise and believe that Islamist movements will never be allowed by domestic and external vested interests to attain or retain power through the ballot box. The Egyptian fiasco, combined with the earlier Algerian example when an Islamist party was denied power by the military in the 1990s after winning an election, is bound to augment the appeal of the extremists' argument.

A segment of this rejectionist camp is also not averse to taking up arms against the "system" that suppresses them as well as against its foreign supporters. It is almost certain that some elements among the disillusioned mainstream Egyptian Islamists will decide to join this militant trend and resort to arms, thus increasing the odds of this volatile region descending into greater anarchy and turmoil. It is not unlikely that Egypt, which had been home to terrorism by fringe Islamist groups in the 1980s and 1990s, will once again see an escalation in such terrorism aimed particularly at high government officials and Western tourists.

This loss for the moderate Islamists will not be limited to Egypt alone. Islamists around the Middle East and beyond will draw the same lessons as do their Egyptian counterparts. With constitutional doors to power closed to them, a segment of them can be expected to resort to violence in increasing numbers. Some of the disillusioned Islamists may also join al-Qaeda-linked transnational terrorist organizations to vent their anger against the traditional supporters of Egypt's military regime, especially the United States, whose Secretary of State made the Orwellian statement that the military coup of July 3, 2013, was a step toward "restoration of democracy" in Egypt. Many of the gains both in the intra-Islamist struggle between moderation and radicalism and in the war on terror are likely to be eroded if a significant number of moderate Islamists give up on the democracy route because they feel that the rules of the game will never be applied to them fairly and move toward extra-constitutional, including violent, paths to gain power and popularity. The Egyptian generals, by removing President Morsi from power, have done a great disservice not only to the cause of democracy but also to that of Islamist moderation in the Middle East.[2] This is likely to come to haunt both the region and the external powers with major interests in the Middle East.

It is also interesting to note the regional reactions to the Egyptian coup. Turkey, the only country in the Muslim Middle East that is a functioning democracy and with a governing party that has Islamist roots, condemned the military takeover in very strong terms. It did so among other things because it does not want the Egyptian episode to influence the attitude of the Turkish military, which the ruling AKP has brought under civilian control after much effort and controversy. Saudi Arabia, worried about the Muslim Brotherhood's combination of Islamism and populism that contradicts its politically quietist version of political Islam, seemed overjoyed by Morsi's ouster and immediately congratulated General Sisi on the military takeover. Additionally, Saudi Arabia and its fellow-members of the GCC, the United Arab Emirates and Kuwait, immediately pledged $12 billion in aid to the new government installed by the Egyptian military in order to shore up Egypt's tottering economy and help prevent the Brotherhood's return to power.

Will the Middle East Implode?

The division of opinion on Egypt between Turkey and Saudi Arabia demonstrates that, notwithstanding their cooperation on Syria, they are strange bedfellows and that their similar anti-Assad postures hide the fundamental differences they have in terms of their long-term views of the Middle East.

The Sunni–Shia divide

The intra-Islamist battle is no longer limited to the one between moderates and radicals within Sunni Islam practiced by the majority of the population in the Middle East. A parallel war has begun to rage between Sunni and Shia radicals, particularly in Iraq, Syria, and Lebanon, where people belonging to the two denominations, divided almost equally in demographic terms, have lived side by side for centuries. This sectarian strife also affects the Arab littoral of the Persian Gulf – Bahrain, eastern Saudi Arabia, and Kuwait in particular – which is home to significant Shia populations living under Sunni monarchical rule.

While the Sunni–Shia rift can be traced back to the first century of Islam, its latest phase owes its origins to the American invasion of Iraq and the consequent change in the sectarian balance of power in that oil-rich country which lies at the heart of the Arab world linking the Fertile Crescent to the Persian Gulf. Although Saddam's repressive regime was not sectarian in the traditional sense of term, it relied heavily upon his kith and kin, who were Sunnis. That the Saddam regime was not sectarian is demonstrated by its harsh and even inhumane treatment of predominantly Sunni Kurds as well as Sunni Arab opponents of the regime. What gave the impression of Sunni dominance was the fact the Arab Shia majority in southern Iraq was the most restive segment, apart from the non-Arab Kurds, of the Iraqi population during Baathist rule, and periodically rose in revolt only to be suppressed with great vehemence by Saddam's forces.

American policy-makers came to view the Iraqi political scene through sectarian lenses in the wake of the invasion that toppled the Saddam regime in 2003. They concluded that the Sunni Arabs were the bad guys and the Shia Arabs were the good guys and launched a policy that favored the latter to the detriment of Sunni interests. This not only precipitated a major Sunni insurgency against the American occupation, it also divided the Arab populace in Iraq along sectarian lines This division was further augmented when the American occupation authorities launched the twin policies of de-Baathification of the civilian bureaucracy and the simultaneous dismantling of the Iraqi armed forces because of their presumed Baathist leanings. These polices led to the near-total collapse of the Iraqi state, forcing both individual Iraqis and entire communities to take refuge in sectarian identities and align themselves with armed sectarian groups in order to ensure the protection for themselves that the state could no longer provide. Consequently, on occasion, sectarian clashes descended into full-fledged warfare.

The hardening of the Sunni–Shia divide increasingly became reflected in the composition of the central government in Baghdad, especially after November 2010, when Nouri al-Maliki of the Shia Dawa party was installed as Prime Minister for the second time, with Iranian support, as the head of a national coalition. Although the Shia bloc itself was fractured among three major groups – Dawa, SCIRI, and the Sadrists – al-Maliki increasingly alienated the Sunni partners in his coalition as he concentrated power in his own hands and those of his henchmen and began to hound out Sunni opponents as soon as American forces departed Iraq at the end of 2011. This strategy boomeranged and, fueled by a sense of Sunni political impotence, led to a renewal in 2012 of the Sunni insurgency that had lain dormant since 2007. Consequently, sectarian killings primarily conducted through suicide bombings especially by al-Qaeda-linked Sunni extremists increased in geometric progressions in 2013, making it one of the bloodiest years in Iraq since the American invasion of 2003.

The Sunni–Shia rift in Iraq was not an isolated event. It both reflected and became intertwined with a region-wide rise in inter-sectarian tension which was given a boost by events connected with the Arab Spring, especially in Bahrain and Syria. The rise of the Shia in Iraq had coincided with the rise of Iranian influence in that country, an unintended consequence of America's removal of Iran's nemesis Saddam Hussein from power. It was, therefore, perceived, or at least touted, by Sunni autocrats around the region led by Saudi Arabia as a part of a deliberate Iranian strategy of establishing a Shia crescent to include Iran and Iraq, both with Shia majorities, Lebanon, where the Shia constitute the largest confessional group and where the Shia Hizbullah plays a major political role, and Syria, where the Assad regime, which drew its support from the Alawites, who are considered an offshoot of Shia Islam, is a close ally of Iran.

Sectarian conflict in Iraq and by extension in Lebanon and Syria, therefore, became a part of the regional cold war between Shia Iran and Wahhabi Saudi Arabia, the two powers that were already contesting the leadership role, as discussed in chapter 4, in the energy-rich Persian Gulf. The predominantly Shia uprising in Bahrain against a Saudi-supported Sunni monarchy and its suppression with the help of Saudi forces added to the tensions between Riyadh and Tehran. Finally, the two powers' involvement in the Syrian civil war on opposite sides has accentuated the perception that the Sunni–Shia divide has now become the principal fault-line in the politics of the Middle East.[3]

While it is true that the sectarian divide has hardened and that Iran is the leading Shia power in the Middle East, it is an exaggeration to argue that this amounts to the creation of a Shia crescent under Iranian tutelage. The Shia in the Middle East are divided between Arabs and Persians with their distinct identities. The Arab Shia are also divided by tribe, nationality, and ideology. Several of the leading Arab Shia figures, including Ayatullah al-Sistani, the leading Iraqi cleric, do not subscribe to the ideology of the ruling clerics in Iran that prescribes active clerical involvement in affairs of state. The rivalry between the Iraqi center of Shia learning, Najaf, and its Iranian counterpart, Qom, adds to the distinctive trajectories of Arab and

Persian Shiism. The increase in Shia political clout in Iraq and Lebanon is largely a reflection of demographic realities and the rise in *Arab* Shia political consciousness and popular mobilization in those countries and not a product of Iranian conspiracy.

As argued in chapter 4, the Syrian–Iranian alliance is driven primarily by strategic factors and not sectarian affinities since the Alawites of Syria are not part of the Shia mainstream and are considered heretical by most Shia. The Saudi and allied attempt to portray an Iranian threat to the Sunni-dominated Middle East via the medium of the Shia crescent serves the purpose of consolidating Sunni support for Saudi Arabia but does not adequately reflect political realities on the ground. Nonetheless, it is very useful to the Saudi regime as a propaganda device, augments the Sunni–Shia division in the Middle East, and makes the volatile nature of the region significantly worse.

Summing up

Forces let loose by the Arab Spring have exacerbated pre-existing problems in the Middle East as well as added new dimensions to them. The specters of state failure, life-and-death struggle over the reversal of the democratization process, the re-radicalization of Islamist movements, the escalation of sectarian strife between Sunnis and Shia, and the intensification of regional rivalries have come to haunt the Middle East simultaneously, increasing the prospects of a major implosion or a series of smaller but interconnected implosions in the region.

The danger of the Middle East descending into region-wide civil strife increases exponentially if you add to these sources of conflict the damage that can be inflicted on the region by the non-resolution of the Israel–Palestine conflict and the fall-out of an attack on Iran's nuclear facilities by Israel or the United States or the two working in tandem with each other. Whilst both these crucial issues have been dealt with in detail in earlier chapters, it is worth dwelling on their likely consequences for the region's future stability.

I believe it is too late to implement a two-state solution for the Israel–Palestine conflict, for reasons analyzed in chapter 3. The real battle likely to be waged on this issue is about the nature of the one-state solution, whether it will be a genuinely bi-national, democratic state with equal rights for all or an apartheid state with one religio-national group dominating the rest of the population. All indications point to the latter outcome, which is bound to result in unending strife that will become increasingly violent and draw in other regional states as well as the major powers. It will also discredit American standing in the region immensely because of Washington's close relations with and support for Israel, right or wrong.

The nuclear question, which is ostensibly portrayed as the dispute over Iran's enrichment rights and its aspiration to clandestinely acquire nuclear weapons capability, is in actual fact related to the fundamental issue of a nuclear balance in the Middle East. This issue can be resolved in only one of two ways: either by the establishment of a MENWFZ that includes both Israel and Iran; or by a state of deterrence between the two nuclear powers that would provide a modicum of stability to the region just as nuclear deterrence between the United States and the Soviet Union did to the global system during the Cold War.[4] Bombing Iran's nuclear facilities will permanently rule out the first option in addition to introducing a high degree of conflict and volatility to the region. Moreover, such a strategy, while postponing the second option temporarily, will ensure its eventual adoption because it will strengthen the Iranian resolve to acquire nuclear weapons and do so publicly and without inhibition. It is time that the major powers, especially the P5+1, which are engaged in nego-tiations with Iran, made up their mind as to which outcome they would prefer.

The bottom line is that if one adds these two issues, Israel–Palestine and the nuclear stand-off between Israel and Iran, to the sources of conflict already exacerbated by the Arab Spring, one finds that the Middle East is sitting on a powder-keg that is likely to implode/explode in multifarious ways. Given the many interconnections among these issues, one cannot rule out chain reactions that may end up engulfing the entire region and threatening energy resources concentrated in the Middle East, and particularly its Persian Gulf sub-region, that are vital to the economic health of Europe and Japan, on the one hand, and China and India, on the other.

Therefore, while there is no simple or categori-cal answer to the question "Will the Middle East Implode?," the odds that this may happen have increased manyfold over the past few years thanks in part to the forces let loose by the uprisings in the Arab world. These have seriously weakened the old order but have not succeeded in establishing an alternative model for the regulation of intra-state and inter-state affairs in the region. Such systemic breakdowns are often precursors to high degrees of volatility and conflict, as the run-up to World War I in Europe demonstrated in unmistakable terms. The Middle East seems to be poised on the cusp of a similar tragedy.

Afterword

Important developments have taken place in relation to two major issues analyzed in the book since the manuscript was completed. These deserve at least brief mention to bring readers up to date.

The Syrian chemical weapons crisis

The first such development, which threatened to lead to a confrontation between the United States and Russia, was the use of chemical weapons (CW) in the Syrian civil war. It almost led to American airstrikes against Syrian targets, including the command and communication centers of the government. The incident that brought this matter to a head was a major CW attack on August 21, 2013 in a suburb of Damascus that, according to estimates which are disputed by Assad and his supporters, left 1,400 people dead. Although UN inspectors allowed into the area confirmed that CW had been used, their brief did not allow them to firmly establish who was responsible. Nonetheless, President Obama, who had announced in August 2012 that the use of CW was a "red line" which when crossed would trigger an American military response, threatened to attack Syrian targets from the air, most probably with cruise missiles. He did this on the assumption, which the administration said was backed by American and allied intelligence, that the Assad regime was responsible for this deployment of CW.

Some quick-footed Russian diplomacy, which built on what seemed to be an off-the-cuff remark by US Secretary of State John Kerry, persuaded the Syrian regime to allow international inspection and the eventual destruction of its CW stockpile, thus averting the immediate danger of an American air attack. Congressional reluctance to provide Obama with the authority to launch such strikes also made the US President amenable to a diplomatic resolution of the crisis. Had the United States made good on its threat to strike Syria, it would have turned out to be a major escalation of the conflict and may have tilted the military balance decisively against the Assad regime. Furthermore, it would have led to an unprecedented confrontation in the post-Cold War era between Washington and Moscow.

However, the danger of such escalation is not yet over, for the unanimously agreed UN Security Council resolution on the issue makes two legally binding demands on Syria: that it disposes of its CW stockpile and that UN-authorized CW experts be given unfettered access to these weapons. In the event of Syrian non-compliance, which can be interpreted in multiple ways given the unsettled situation in the country, the resolution authorizes the Council to take action under Chapter VII of the UN Charter. What such action may amount to is left unclear because of lack of agreement on this issue between Russia, which is adamantly opposed to military action, and the United States, which wants the military option left on the table. This means that while non-compliance will not automatically trigger military strikes, for such action will have to be authorized by another vote of the Security Council, it does leave the option open for American and allied strikes with or without Security Council endorsement.

It became clear as the crisis developed that the Obama administration was reluctant to launch an attack on Syria in part because of Western apprehensions that a serious weakening of the country's regime could redound to the benefit of extremist jihadi groups linked to al-Qaeda that have been at the forefront of the fight against Assad but also have transnational anti-Western agendas. Unwilling to countenance such a situation, the United States agreed to settle for a diplomatic solution to the crisis that the Russians, afraid that the CW stockpile might fall into the hands of Islamist extremists if Assad were toppled, persuaded the Syrian regime to accept as well.

While the CW crisis may have blown over for the time being, its resolution leaves intact the fundamental problem facing the Syrian polity: namely, an end to the civil war – negotiated or otherwise – that would leave the state structure largely intact while removing the family and sectarian dictatorship that has ruled the country for the past four decades. This appears an increasingly improbable goal given the fact that the regime and the state in Syria have become virtually synonymous. The longer the civil war goes on and the greater the external involvement in this conflict, the less likely it is that a post-conflict Syria will emerge within its current borders. This opens up frightening possibilities of state disintegration not only for Syria but also for its neighbors Lebanon and Iraq, which are even more divided on the basis of sect, confession, and ethnicity. Syria's disintegration is likely to signal the unraveling of the entire Sykes–Picot regional order imposed on the Arab parts of the Ottoman Empire by Britain and France at the end of World War I.

The Iranian "charm offensive"

The second major development was the launching of what is popularly called the Iranian "charm offensive" by the new Iranian government under President Hassan Rouhani that took office in August 2013. It reached its zenith a month later when Rouhani, accompanied by his suave and sophisticated Foreign Minister, Javad Zarif, visited New York to speak at the UN General Assembly. Rouhani adopted a very conciliatory tone both in his General Assembly speech and in an op-ed published in the *Washington Post* a few days before his arrival in New York.[1] He stated categorically that Iran would never pursue a nuclear weapons option and that this was not a part of its security doctrine. He assured the international community that Iran was willing to set its concerns about the country's nuclear program at rest by negotiating on this issue seriously with the P5+1. Rouhani's visit to the

United Nations was capped on his way to the airport by a cordial 15-minute telephone conversation he had with President Obama. That both Iran and the P5+1 were seriously committed to negotiations under the changed circumstances was demonstrated by the meeting that Foreign Minister Zarif had with the foreign ministers of the P5+1 and the EU foreign policy chief, Catherine Ashton, in New York and again separately with US Secretary of State John Kerry. According to newspaper reports, the vibes at and after these meeting were very positive.

Rouhani's statements and Obama's overtures, in the form of a letter to the Iranian President before the latter's sojourn to New York and the above-mentioned telephone call, have perceptibly changed the atmospherics surrounding US–Iran relations. However, the two sides' positions on Iran's uranium enrichment program and the lifting of economic sanctions on the country continue to diverge widely, as demonstrated by Rouhani's statement in Tehran not long after his return from New York that Iran is willing to discuss "details" of uranium enrichment but not its right to enrich uranium guaranteed by the NPT.[2] Although the changed atmosphere may help close the gap to some extent, it remains to be seen whether a mutually acceptable solution that satisfies both parties'

Afterword

minimum demands can be reached within a reasonable time-frame. Iran is obviously in a hurry to close the nuclear file because of the dire economic straits it finds itself in as a result of the unprecedented economic sanctions imposed upon it. However, there are certain long-standing constants shaping its security environment, which we discussed in detail in chapter 5, that require that Tehran not abjure the nuclear weapons option totally and for ever.

There are also many potential "spoilers" on both sides waiting to discredit as a sham the process of rapprochement launched with Rouhani's election. Hardliners in Iran, although currently muzzled by the Supreme Leader, who has thrown his support behind Rouhani's overtures to the United States, are hovering in the wings and at the first signs of discord between the two sides will once again raise the banner of "no negotiations with the Great Satan." Similarly, right-wing constituencies in the United States, and more particularly the Israel lobby led by AIPAC, which has enormous clout with Congress, have already launched a frontal attack on the fledgling process of Iranian–American rapprochement. They have done so by portraying Rouhani as a dishonest double-dealer and by representing Obama as a naïve and weak President who can be easily tricked by the wily Iranian to make concessions that

170

would leave Tehran's nuclear weapons program intact.

Israeli Prime Minister Benjamin Netanyahu, visibly desperate at the prospects of an American–Iranian rapprochement, which would considerably reduce Israel's strategic value to the United States, personally led the charge against any softening of the American position on Iran. In his speech to the UN General Assembly a week after Rouhani's oration, he warned Obama not to be deceived by the Iranian President, whom he called a "wolf in sheep's clothing," and to keep the pressure on Iran until the latter agrees to totally abandon its uranium enrichment program. Netanyahu combined this exhortation aimed at the United States with a near-explicit threat that if it comes to it, Israel intends to go it alone and take out the Iranian nuclear facilities in order to deny Iran nuclear weapons capability. It is indeed ironic that Israel, which is the sole nuclear weapons power in the Middle East and wants to maintain its nuclear monopoly at all costs, should threaten a member of the NPT, which may or may not be aiming to achieve nuclear weapons capability, in order not only to prevent Iran from acquiring that capability but also to prevent it from enriching uranium for peaceful purposes under IAEA safeguards.

Afterword

But this is not a matter for irony or sarcasm because the Israel lobby in collusion with the anti-Obama right wing forces in the US Congress is quite capable of derailing the nascent rapprochement between Washington and Tehran. The easiest way to do so is to put pressure on members of Congress not to lift the crippling sanctions on Iran enshrined in acts passed by Congress over the past few years. These are the most severe of the plethora of sanctions imposed on Iran by the UN Security Council, the EU, the US Congress, and executive orders of the American President. If the anti-Iran lobby is able to prevent the repeal of these sanctions legislated by Congress, Obama will be left with just "peanuts" to offer Iran in exchange for the latter's "diamonds" – a sure way to send the wrong signal to Tehran.[3]

The Iranian negotiators will also be working under constraints imposed upon them by domestic factors. These include a firm commitment given by all Iranian governments, including Rouhani's, that Iran will never give up its right to enrich uranium within the country for peaceful purposes, a right guaranteed under the NPT. While such enrichment under the treaty will be undertaken using IAEA safeguards, some of Iran's P5+1 interlocutors may not perceive it as a satisfactory arrangement because it will still leave both nuclear material and know-how for nuclear weapons in Iranian possession. Moreover, the undercurrent of Iranian nationalism that demands that Tehran must keep its nuclear weapons option open is also likely to work against an accommodation with the Western powers. Although the current Iranian government, given the dire economic situation facing the population, may be willing to give up this option in exchange for the lifting of economic sanctions, it may not be able to carry the country with it.

In short, there are too many roadblocks in the way of solving the Iranian nuclear issue that could quickly abort the process of rapprochement begun by Rouhani and Obama. Obama's statement after his meeting with Netanyahu on September 30, 2013, that he would take "no options off the table, including military action, to prevent Iran from obtaining a nuclear weapon," has once again roiled the Iranian leadership, who see it as an unwarranted threat in the context of the emerging thaw in the relations between Iran and the United States.[4] Moreover, as discussed in chapter 5, it is naïve to expect a satisfactory solution to this problem without a radical improvement in the overall relationship between Tehran and Washington that neutralizes the mistrust and antagonism that has characterized it for the past several decades. It is this mistrust and antagonism that provide Iran the motivation to preserve its nuclear weapons option, and not the other way around.

The Arab winter

Events in the Arab Spring countries continue to make one despondent. Egypt, as stated in earlier chapters, is once again firmly under the boot of the military and security services that had formed the bulwark of the Mubarak dictatorship. Even Tunisia, which appeared to have survived multiple crises, has succumbed to the obduracy of the secular opposition and the extremism of salafi groups who have targeted opposition leaders for assassination. The moderately Islamist Ennahda government has been forced to offer its resignation and agree to hand over power to a neutral, "non-political" government. The installation of such a government is expected to lead to the return of the opposition members to the Constituent Assembly that they had been boycotting, followed by the writing of a constitution which will pave the way for fresh elections to Parliament. While this outcome is better than the scenario that unfolded in neighboring Egypt, it indicates that the rules of the democratic game – above all, respect for electoral outcomes – have not yet been fully internalized by political actors in that country.

Libya and Yemen continue to be beset by instability and insecurity, and Syria is headed down the Iraqi path of sectarian strife and indiscriminate killings, with dismemberment a distinct possibility. Bahrain's democracy movement remains suppressed, with activists prosecuted in kangaroo courts that sentence them to long terms in prison. All this goes on with the active collusion of Saudi Arabia and the passive complicity of the United States. Saudi Arabia, the leader of the counter-revolutionary brigade, seems to be riding high currently with the visible turning of the democracy tide, as demonstrated especially by the military's overthrow of the Morsi government in Egypt, a move openly applauded and financially supported by the Saudi establishment. The monarchical regimes in Morocco and Jordan have also been encouraged by the failure of the democracy movements among their neighbors to take steps to shut down political openings that had been forced on them by the fear of the demonstration effects of earlier uprisings in the Arab world.

The Palestinians, divided among themselves and

with their residual patrimony increasingly colonized by Jewish settlers, seem to be simultaneously in a state of disarray and on the verge of a major uprising that could eclipse the first two *intifadas* in terms of fervor and ferocity and further destabilize neighboring countries. As we have argued in chapter 3, the two-state solution to the Israel–Palestine conflict is dead but a one-state solution is unlikely to be born without major violence and bloodletting.[5]

To conclude, it is doubtful that we will hear much good news from the Arab world for a considerable length of time.

October 9, 2013

Further Reading

A plethora of books and articles on the Middle East have appeared in recent years, especially after the tragic events of September 11, 2001. Much of this literature is of uneven quality and some of it is propagandistic in nature. Therefore, one has to sift through these publications carefully in order to select those that shed light relatively objectively on the current situation in the Middle East. This is what I will try to do in this section.

James L. Gelvin's *The Modern Middle East: A History* (New York: Oxford University Press, 2011) is a good overview of how the forces associated with global modernity have shaped the social, economic, cultural, and political life of the region over the course of the past 500 years. This can be usefully supplemented by David Fromkin's *A Peace to End All Peace, 20th Anniversary Edition: The*

Fall of the Ottoman Empire and the Creation of the Modern Middle East (New York: Holt Paperbacks, 2009). It deals with the vivisection of the Middle East at the end of World War I under the guise of the League of Nations Mandates and demonstrates how current conflicts in the region are rooted in this division undertaken for the convenience of imperial powers, primarily Britain and France.

James L. Gelvin's *The Arab Uprisings: What Everyone Needs to Know* (New York: Oxford University Press, 2012) provides a basic introduction to the uprisings. Readers who would like to delve a little more deeply into the subject will find Marc Lynch's *The Arab Uprising: The Unfinished Revolutions of the New Middle East* (New York: Public Affairs, 2013) very useful. Another very good read in a more racy style is Robin Wright's *Rock the Casbah: Rage and Rebellion across the Islamic World* (New York: Simon and Schuster, 2011).

Chapter 2 on the Islamist challenge should be read in conjunction with my own *The Many Faces of Political Islam: Religion and Politics in the Muslim World* (Ann Arbor: University of Michigan Press, 2008), which argues that political Islam is not a monolith and its manifestations are highly context-specific and embrace a wide variety of ideologies and strategies. Readers interested in Islamist movements in the Arab world will find it useful to read Nathan Brown's *When Victory Is Not an Option: Islamist Movements in Arab Politics* (Ithaca, NY: Cornell University Press, 2012).

On the Israel–Palestine conflict, especially the current deadlock, which is the subject matter of chapter 3, the reader should begin with Rashid Khalidi's *Palestinian Identity: The Construction of Modern National Consciousness* (New York: Columbia University Press, 2009) and then move on to Virginia Tilley's *The One-State Solution: A Breakthrough for Peace in the Israeli–Palestinian Deadlock* (Ann Arbor: University of Michigan Press, reprint edn, 2010) and Yehouda Shenhav's *Beyond the Two-State Solution: A Jewish Political Essay* (Cambridge: Polity, 2012).

Chapter 4 on regional and global rivalries in the context of the Arab uprisings of 2011–13 deals with contemporary issues, and no book-length study that adequately covers the subject is available so far. However, there are several highly informative articles that are worth reading, including my own "The Arab Spring: Its Geostrategic Significance," *Middle East Policy*, Fall 2012, pp. 84–97, and Mehran Kamrava's "The Arab Spring and the Saudi-Led Counterrevolution," *Orbis*, Winter

2012, pp. 96–104. The International Crisis Group's *Syria's Metastasising Conflicts* (Middle East Report No. 143, June 27, 2013) provides a very balanced analysis of the Syrian civil war, including the involvement of external powers.

David Patrikarakos's *Nuclear Iran: The Birth of an Atomic State* (London: I.B. Tauris, 2012) provides good background to the Iranian nuclear program discussed in chapter 5. Since Iran's nuclear aspirations cannot be understood in isolation from Israel's nuclear weapons capabilities, Avner Cohen's *The Worst-Kept Secret: Israel's Bargain with the Bomb* (New York: Columbia University Press, 2012) is essential reading for those interested in further exploring this subject. For an eloquent argument that nuclear deterrence between Israel and Iran will provide stability in the Middle East, read Kenneth N. Waltz's "Why Iran Should Get the Bomb: Nuclear Balancing Would Mean Stability," *Foreign Affairs*, July/August 2012, pp. 2–5. Trita Parsi's *A Single Roll of the Dice: Obama's Diplomacy with Iran* (New Haven, CT: Yale University Press, reprint edn, 2012) provides a very sensible and sobering analysis of the current state of relations between the United States and Iran.

Chapter 6 deals, among other issues, with the

battle between the fringe militant Islamists and the mainstream constitutionalist Islamists for the soul of political Islam. A must-read for those interested in this subject is Fawaz Gerges's *The Rise and Fall of al-Qaeda* (New York: Oxford University Press, 2011). Readers interested in further exploring the contemporary manifestation of the Sunni–Shia rift analyzed in this chapter will find much useful material in Geneive Abdo's *The New Sectarianism: The Arab Uprisings and the Rebirth of the Shi'a–Sunni Divide* (The Saban Center for Middle East Policy, Brookings Institution, Washington, DC, Analysis Paper Number 29, April 2013). For the likely long-term impact of the Egyptian coup of July 2013 that unseated President Morsi of the Muslim Brotherhood, see Khaled M. Abou El Fadl, "The Perils of a 'People's Coup,'" *New York Times*, July 7, 2013.

Notes

Chapter 1 After the Arab Spring

1 For a balanced analysis from an American establishment perspective of the costs and benefits of military action against Iran's nuclear facilities, see the report produced by the Iran Project titled *Weighing Benefits and Costs of Military Action Against Iran*, published in September 2012, at *http://www.scribd.com/doc/106806148/IranReport-092412-Final#fullscreen* (accessed August 23, 2013).

2 "Naftali Bennet, Israel's Economy Minister, Says Palestinian Statehood is 'Dead-End,'" *Huffington Post*, June 17, 2013, at *http://www.huffingtonpost.com/2013/06/17/naftali-bennet-palestinian-state_n_3453048.html* (accessed August 23, 2013).

3 For a discussion of the pros and cons of Islamist parties coming to power in the wake of the Arab uprisings, see Marina Ottaway and Marwan Muasher, *Islamist Parties in Power: A Work in Progress*, Carnegie

Endowment for International Peace, Washington, DC, May 23, 2012, at *http://carnegieendowment. org/2012/05/23/islamist-parties-in-power-work-in-progress/aw7x#* (accessed August 23, 2013).

Chapter 2 The Islamist Challenge

1 The argument covered in the first two paragraphs of this chapter is made in detail in my *The Many Faces of Political Islam: Religion and Politics in the Muslim World* (Ann Arbor: University of Michigan Press, 2008), chapters 1 and 2.

2 Fawaz Gerges, *The Far Enemy: Why Jihad Went Global* (New York: Cambridge University Press, 2005).

3 For a comprehensive study of Qutb's ideas, see John Calvert, *Sayyid Qutb and the Origins of Radical Islamism* (New York: Columbia University Press, 2010).

4 Gilles Kepel, *The Prophet and the Pharaoh: Muslim Extremism in Egypt* (London: Saqi Books, 1985), p. 63.

5 Fawaz Gerges, *The Rise and Fall of al-Qaeda* (New York: Oxford University Press, 2011).

6 For details of this argument, see Mohammed Ayoob, "American Policy Toward the Persian Gulf: Strategies, Effectiveness, and Consequences," in Mehran Kamrava, *International Politics of the Persian Gulf* (Syracuse, NY: Syracuse University Press, 2011); also see Max Fisher, "Beyond Secret Drones: The Roots of the Awkward, Improbable, Contradictory

US–Saudi Relationship," *Washington Post*, February 6, 2013, at *http://www.washingtonpost.com/blogs/ worldviews/wp/2013/02/06/beyond-secret-drones-the-roots-of-the-awkward-improbable-contradic tory-u-s-saudi-relationship/* (accessed August 26, 2013).

7 For details, see Stephane Lacroix, *Awakening Islam: The Politics of Religious Dissent in Contemporary Saudi Arabia* (Cambridge, MA: Harvard University Press, 2011); and Thomas Hegghammer, *Jihad in Saudi Arabia: Violence and Pan-Islamism since 1979* (New York: Cambridge University Press, 2010).

8 Frederic Wehrey, *The Precarious Ally: Bahrain's Impasse and US Policy*, The Carnegie Papers, Washington, DC, February 2013, at *http://carnegie endowment.org/files/bahrain_impasse.pdf* (accessed August 26, 2013).

9 Reuel Marc Gerecht, *The Islamic Paradox: Shiite Clerics, Sunni Fundamentalists, and the Coming of Arab Democracy* (Washington, DC: AEI Press, 2004).

10 Matthew Duss and Peter Juul, *The Fractured Shia of Iraq: Understanding the Tension within Iraq's Majority* (Center for American Progress, January 2009), at *http://www.americanprogress.org/wp-con tent/uploads/issues/2009/01/pdf/shia_elections.pdf* (accessed August 26, 2013).

Chapter 3 Deadlock over Palestine

1 Shaul Mishal and Avraham Sela, *The Palestinian Hamas: Vision, Violence, and Coexistence* (New

York: Columbia University Press, 2000), p. 18; Robert Dreyfuss, *Devil's Game: How the United States Helped Unleash Fundamentalist Islam* (New York: Metropolitan Books, 2005), p. 191. Tamar Hausman, "US Ambassador Says 'Israel Encouraged Islamists in Bid to Dampen Palestinian Nationalism,'" *Haaretz*, December 21, 2001, at *http://www.haaretz.com/u-s-ambassador-says-israel-encouraged-islamists-in-bid-to-dampen-palestinian-nationalism-1.77916* (accessed August 27, 2013).

2 Avi Shlaim, "Obama and Israel: The Pessimistic Perspective," *The Antonian*, Michaelmas Term 2010, p. 7, at *http://www.sant.ox.ac.uk/Antonian_Michaelmas2010.pdf* (accessed August 27, 2013).

3 Harriett Sherwood, "Population of Jewish Settlements in West Bank up 15,000 in a Year," *Guardian*, July 26, 2012, at *http://www.theguardian.com/world/2012/jul/26/jewish-population-west-bank-up* (accessed August 27, 2013).

4 For example, Mousa Abu Marzook, "What Hamas is Seeking," *Washington Post*, January 31, 2006, at *http://www.washingtonpost.com/wp-dyn/content/article/2006/01/30/AR2006013001209.html* (accessed August 27, 2013).

5 See "Peace Now's Settlement Watch Report: 2011 a Record Year for West Bank Settlement Construction," *Americans for Peace Now*, January 10, 2012, at *http://peacenow.org/entries/peace_nows_settlement_watch_report_2011_a_record_year_for_west_bank_settlement_construction* (accessed August 27, 2013) for settlement construction in the West Bank; and Nir

Hasson, "Construction in Jerusalem Neighborhoods beyond Green Line Peaked in 2012," *Haaretz*, January 3, 2013, at *http://www.haaretz.com/news/national/construction-in-jerusalem-neighborhoods-beyond-green-line-peaked-in-2012-1.491549* (accessed August 27, 2013) for East Jerusalem.

6 For the influence of the Israel lobby and the distortions it has introduced in American policy toward the Middle East, see John J. Mearsheimer and Stephen W. Walt, *The Israel Lobby and US Foreign Policy* (New York: Farrar, Straus and Giroux, 2008).

7 *http://www.pewglobal.org/2012/05/08/chapter-5-views-of-the-united-states-and-israel/* (accessed August 27, 2013).

8 For details, see *http://www.brookings.edu/~/media/research/files/reports/2012/5/21%20egyptian%20elections%20poll%20telhami/egypt_poll_results* (accessed August 27, 2013).

9 Naftali Bennet, Israel's Economy Minister, Says Palestinian Statehood is 'Dead-End,'" *Huffington Post*, June 17, 2013, at *http://www.huffingtonpost.com/2013/06/17/naftali-bennet-palestinian-state_n_3453048.html* (accessed August 23, 2013).

Chapter 4 Regional and Global Rivalries

1 Marina Ottaway, "Who will Save Egypt? Cairo's Economic Disaster and Those Fighting to Fix It," *Foreign Affairs*, June 30, 2013, at *http://www.*

foreignaffairs.com/articles/139543/marina-ottaway/ who-will-save-egypt (accessed August 30, 2013).

2 David D. Kirkpatrick and Mayy El Sheikh, "Morsi Spurned Deals, Seeing Military as Tamed," *New York Times*, July 6, 2013, at *http://www.nytimes. com/2013/07/07/world/middleeast/morsi-spurned- deals-to-the-end-seeing-the-military-as-tamed. html?ref=global-home&_r=0*; David D. Kirkpatrick and Kareem Fahim, "Brotherhood Says US Diplomats Urged It to Accept Ouster of Morsi," *New York Times*, July 7, 2013, at *http://www. nytimes.com/2013/07/08/world/middleeast/egypt. html?ref=middleeast* (both accessed August 30, 2013).

3 For details, see Stephen W. Day, *Regionalism and Rebellion in Yemen: A Troubled National Union* (New York: Cambridge University Press, 2012).

4 Gregory Johnsen, *The Last Refuge: Yemen, al-Qaeda, and America's War in Arabia* (New York: W.W. Norton, 2012).

5 Patrick Cockburn, "After the Euphoria: On the Arab Uprisings," *The Nation*, October 16, 2012, at *http://www.thenation.com/article/170611/after- euphoria-arab-uprisings?page=full* (accessed August 30, 2013).

6 This is well documented in two major works originally published in the 1960s: Patrick Seale, *The Struggle for Syria* (New Haven: Yale University Press, 1987), and Malcolm Kerr, *The Arab Cold War* (New York: Oxford University Press, 3rd edn, 1971).

7 C.J. Chivers and Eric Schmitt, "Arms Airlift to Syria Rebels Expands, with C.I.A. Aid," *New York Times*, March 24, 2013, at *http://www.nytimes.com/2013/03/25/world/middleeast/arms-airlift-to-syrian-rebels-expands-with-cia-aid.html?ref=global-home&_r=0* (accessed August 30, 2013).

8 Mark Mazzetti, C.J. Chivers, and Eric Schmitt, "Taking Outsize Role in Syria, Qatar Funnels Arms to Rebels," *New York Times*, June 29, 2013, at *http://www.nytimes.com/2013/06/30/world/middleeast/sending-missiles-to-syrian-rebels-qatar-muscles-in.html?ref=global-home&_r=0* (accessed August 30, 2013).

9 "Syrian Crisis 'Could Kill 100,000 Next Year,'" *Guardian*, December 30, 2012, at *http://www.guardian.co.uk/world/2012/dec/30/syrian-crisis-could-kill-100000* (accessed August 30, 2013).

10 Paul Owen, "UN Envoy Says Arming Rebels 'Not the Answer,'" *Guardian*, March 29, 2013, at *http://www.guardian.co.uk/world/middle-east-live/2013/mar/29/un-envoy-says-arming-rebels-not-the-answer-live?INTCMP=SRCH* (accessed August 30, 2013).

11 Frederic Wehrey, "The Precarious Ally: Bahrain's Impasse and US Policy," *Carnegie Endowment for International Peace*, February 6, 2013, at *http://carnegieendowment.org/2013/02/06/precarious-ally-bahrain-s-impasse-and-u.s.-policy/fayh* (accessed August 30, 2013).

Chapter 5 Iran and "the Bomb"

1 Seyed Hossein Mousavian, "Twelve Major Consequences of Sanctions on Iran," *Al-Monitor*, May 3, 2013, at *http://www.al-monitor.com/pulse/ originals/2013/04/iran-sanctions-consequences-list.html?utm_source=&utm_medium=email&utm_ campaign=7138* (accessed August 30, 2013).

2 "How Close is Iran to Having a Nuclear Bomb?," *Economist*, June 26, 2013, at *http://www.economist. com/blogs/economist-explains/2013/06/economist-explains-17* (accessed August 30, 2013).

3 James Risen, "Ghosts of Iraq Haunting CIA in Tackling Iran," *New York Times*, March 31, 2012, at *http://www.nytimes.com/2012/04/01/world/mid dleeast/assessing-iran-but-thinking-about-iraq. html?pagewanted=all* (accessed August 30, 2013).

4 James R. Clapper, Director of National Intelligence, April 11, 2013, at *http://www.dni.gov/files/docu-ments/Intelligence%20Reports/2013%20WW TA%20US%20IC%20SFR%20%20HPSCI%20 11%20Apr%202013.pdf* (accessed August 30, 2013). Emphasis added.

5 Avner Cohen, *The Worst-Kept Secret: Israel's Bargain with the Bomb* (New York: Columbia University Press, 2012).

6 David Patrikarakos, *Nuclear Iran: The Birth of an Atomic State* (London: I.B. Tauris, 2012), p. 55.

7 Zubeida Malik, "The Man Who Turned Iran Nuclear", *BBC News Middle East*, March 28,

2013, at *http://www.bbc.co.uk/news/world-middle-east-21938310* (accessed August 30, 2013).

8 James Dobbins, "Negotiating with Iran," at *http://www.rand.org/content/dam/rand/pubs/testimonies/2007/RAND_CT293.pdf* (accessed August 30, 2013).

9 Ehud Barak, "Interview," *Charlie Rose*, November 15, 2011, at *http://www.youtube.com/watch?v=KSKXQl1QhLw* (accessed September 3 2013).

10 Hossein Mousavian interview with Christiane Amanpour on CNN, May 23, 2012, quoted in Hossein Mousavian, "Iran, the US and Weapons of Mass Destruction," *Survival* 54(5), October–November 2012, p. 191.

11 Iran Project, *Weighing Benefits and Costs of Military Action against Iran*, 2012, at *http://www.wilsoncenter.org/sites/default/files/IranReport_091112_FINAL.pdf* (accessed August 30, 2013).

12 Shibley Telhami and Steven Kull, "Preventing a Nuclear Iran, Peacefully," *International Herald Tribune*, January 15, 2012, at *http://www.nytimes.com/2012/01/16/opinion/preventing-a-nuclear-iran-peacefully.html* (accessed August 30, 2013).

13 Patricia M. Lewis, "A Middle East Free of Nuclear Weapons: Possible, Probable or Pipe-Dream?," *International Affairs* 89(2), March 2013, p. 441.

14 For an eloquent plea on these lines see Trita Parsi, *A Single Roll of the Dice* (New Haven, CT: Yale University Press, reprint edn, 2012).

Chapter 6 Will the Middle East Implode?

1 Khaled M. Abou El Fadl, "The Perils of a 'People's Coup,'" *New York Times*, July 7, 2013, at *http://www.nytimes.com/2013/07/08/opinion/the-perils-of-a-peoples-coup.html?ref=global* (accessed September 2, 2013).

2 Ed Husain, "Egypt Risks the Fire of Radicalism," *New York Times*, July 3, 2013, at *http://www.nytimes.com/2013/07/04/opinion/global/egypt-risks-the-fire-of-radicalism.html?pagewanted=all* (accessed September 2, 2013).

3 Geneive Abdo, *The New Sectarianism: The Arab Uprisings and the Rebirth of the Shi'a–Sunni Divide* (The Saban Center for Middle East Policy, Brookings Institution, Washington, DC, Analysis Paper Number 29, April 2013), at *http://www.brookings.edu/~/media/research/files/papers/2013/04/sunni%20shia%20abdo/sunni%20shia%20abdo.pdf* (accessed September 2, 2013).

4 For the virtues of deterrence between Israel and Iran in the Middle East, see the analysis by the leading structural realist scholar of the twentieth century, the late Kenneth N. Waltz, in his last major article "Why Iran Should Get the Bomb: Nuclear Balancing Would Mean Stability," *Foreign Affairs* 91(4), July/August 2012, pp. 2–5.

Afterword

1 Hassan Rouhani, "Why Iran Seeks Constructive Engagement," *Washington Post*, September 19, 2013, at *http://www.washingtonpost.com/opinions/president-of-iran-hassan-rouhani-time-to-engage/2013/09/19/4d2da564-213e-11e3-966c-9c4293c47ebe_story.html* (accessed October 3, 2013).

2 "Rouhani: Iran Will Discuss 'Details' of Uranium Enrichment, But Not Its Rights," *Washington Post*, October 2, 2013, at *http://www.washingtonpost.com/world/middle_east/rouhani-iran-will-discuss-nuclear-details-but-rights-non-negotiable/2013/10/02/d8894ade-2b82-11e3-b141-298f46539716_story.html* (accessed October 3, 2013).

3 Paul Lewis, "Hopes Raised for US–Iran Talks But Hawks in Congress Threaten Any Deal," *Guardian*, October 3, 2013, at *http://www.theguardian.com/world/2013/oct/03/us-iran-talks-threatened-congress-sanctions* (accessed October 3, 2013).

4 Mark Landler, "Discussing Iran, Obama and Netanyahu Display Unity," *New York Times*, September 30, 2013, at *http://www.nytimes.com/2013/10/01/us/politics/tensions-over-iran-seem-to-ebb-between-netanyahu-and-obama.html?_r=0* (accessed October 3, 2013).

5 For an incisive analysis, see Ian S. Lustick, "Two-State Illusion," *New York Times*, September 14, 2013, at *http://www.nytimes.com/2013/09/15/opinion/sunday/two-state-illusion.html?pagewanted=all* (accessed October 3, 2013).